FEDERAL INDIA

FEDERAL INDIA

BY

COLONEL K. N. HAKSAR, C.I.E.

AND

K. M. PANIKKAR

GYAN

Published by

Gyan Publishing House
5, Ansari Road
Daryaganj, New Delhi-110002
Phone: 011-47034999, 9811692060
E-mail: books@gyanbooks.com

Distribution Network
gyanbooks.com
India, USA, Canada, UK, Australia

ISBN: 978-81-212-7264-3 (HB)
First Published, 1930

2nd Impression 2024

Printed at: Gyan Press, Delhi.

FEDERAL INDIA
Author: K. N. HAKSAR, K. M. PANIKKAR

FEDERAL INDIA

FEDERAL INDIA

BY

COLONEL K. N. HAKSAR C.I.E.

POLITICAL MEMBER OF THE GWALIOR GOVERNMENT
DELEGATE TO THE ROUND TABLE CONFERENCE

AND

K. M. PANIKKAR

DEPUTY DIRECTOR, SPECIAL ORGANIZATION OF
THE CHAMBER OF PRINCES

MARTIN HOPKINSON LTD.
23 SOHO SQUARE LONDON
1930

PREFACE

India presents a baffling problem which may well tax all the latent resources of British statesmanship. There is a clash of wills between the two peoples—British and Indian: the spokesmen of the one convinced that not only its own interests, but also those of the other, require that that other shall yet abide *in statu pupillari*; those of the other equally convinced that it will best discharge all its responsibilities in a state of emancipation. Both rely upon facts honestly maintained to be unquestionable, but of which the assessment as to future possibilities, at any rate, belongs to the realm of speculation. The one is, however, not disposed to allow any element of speculation in matters of hard practical politics; the other, arguing alike from innate faith and examples not very dissimilar, refuses to admit that there is any room for speculative uncertainty in a forecast of the ultimate issue.

Nevertheless, the problem of the attainment of political freedom by India is not free from complexities. And yet the essence of the problem is capable of the simplest solution, if only a subjective estimate of the essentials of human nature, in the twentieth century, provide its basis. The 'open sesame' would be found in the faculty on which Gordon Pasha laid so much emphasis or for which, possibly, he prayed. But, assuming that the crisis which has undoubtedly arisen in India enables the statesmen of England to 'get into the skins' of their fellow-subjects of British India and their friendly neighbours of Indian India, the satisfactory adjustment of the country's internal relations would still require much deep thought and patient investigation.

If England is to fulfil her mission in India, consistently with a sagacious discharge of her duty to the Empire of which she is at once the cement and the apex, no makeshift expedients will achieve that end. No self-regarding scheme, or one that can be impugned as less just to one interest than another, will set India on the path to her destined and promised goal. Every consideration incidental to the problem will have to be nicely balanced and the lessons of history and of the constitutions of many countries pressed into service for the necessary survey. The effect on the Indian mind of the leading events of the last thirty years, in conjunction with that of the inculcation of British ideals of Liberty and Justice for nearly a century, will have to be appreciated. And the probability, in an autonomous India, of discord resulting from differences of religion and culture will have to be sincerely appraised. Account will have to be taken of the example of America, as also of the fact that in Britain Celts and Saxons, Christians and Jews, Huguenots and Jesuits have, in course of time, all become welded in a homogeneous Nation. Whatever their differences of language, and whatever their countries of origin, the inhabitants of India are one people and have dwelt together sufficiently long to be one race and nationality. *Réchauffés* of ancient arguments derived from apparent differences must, therefore, be assessed at their true value.

The position in regard to the Indian States is, however, on a different footing. Their insistence on individual autonomy is only a manifestation of 'regional particularism.' Assuming that Hyderabad and Mysore could be abolished, they would still want to be separate provinces and to govern themselves as Sindh and Andhra wish to be and to do, even though they have for so long been parts of larger administrative units. But, apart from the sociological fact of such particularistic tendency, of which history provides so many examples, there are, in the case of the states, the solemn pledges of England which England must respect, even while attempting to fulfil her mission in India.

The object of this Essay is sufficiently explained by its title; it is to discuss and suggest solutions of the problem arising from a federation of Indian States with British India.

So far, the federal solution of India's problems has been discussed purely from the point of view of the political organisation of British India. Sir Frederick Whyte in his interesting monograph entitled 'India, a Federation?' prepared at the suggestion of the Government of India, discussed the question of federating the provinces into a British Indian Commonwealth. The provinces of British India are at the present time merely administrative units; and unless the whole machinery of government is to be reconstituted, they will remain so, though in the future much more extensive powers may be delegated to them.

The problem that we have attempted to discuss in the present volume is altogether different; it is the organic union of the sovereign states of India with the British Indian Government. If such a union is to be achieved, it *can only be on a federal basis*. A unitary centralised government for the whole of India including the states is impossible, as the Crown is bound by its treaties and engagements with Indian rulers to protect and maintain their sovereignty. This guarantee of the sovereign rights of the states is the fundamental and governing factor in any proposal for the intimate association of states with British India. What we have attempted is to analyse the conditions of closer co-operation, and to discuss the problem that will face both British India and the states if Greater India is to come into being. The correspondence between the Prime

Minister and Sir John Simon and the historic declaration of the Viceroy made it clear that one of the main objects of the Round Table Conference would be to explore this complicated problem. It is hoped that this study, incomplete as it is, may prove to be of some help in the desired exploration.

K. N. H.
K. M. P.

SIMLA,
August 18, 1930.

CONTENTS

THE sensible question to ask about a book is obviously whether it makes some contribution to a clearer understanding of our situation by adding or reaffirming important considerations and the inferences to be made from these. Such books could be set off against those that were but expressions of vague discontent or emulation, or denunciations of things because they are as they are or are not as they are not. I have personally little confidence in those who cry lo here or lo there. It is premature to advocate any wide sweeping reconstruction of the social order, although experiments and suggestions should be encouraged. What we need first is a change of heart and a chastened mood which will permit an ever-increasing number of people to see things as they are, in the light of what they have been and what they might be.

JAMES HARVEY ROBINSON
The Mind in the Making

FEDERAL INDIA

CHAPTER I

CENTRIFUGAL FORCES IN INDIA

THE political experience of Great Britain will soon meet at the conference table the national aspirations of India for the purpose of evolving a permanent and workable constitution for a self-governing India. The occasion should provide the crucial test, not only of the statesmanship of the representatives of Great Britain, but also of the practical wisdom and patriotic insight of the representatives of India. If anything tangible is to result from the conference it is necessary that both parties should approach the problem, not merely with goodwill and in a spirit of co-operation, but with a clear understanding of the issues for which a solution is sought. Much spade work has to be done before the conference actually meets, and ideas should be clarified and put into a practicable shape, so that the collective wisdom of the conference could criticise, test and select from the results of the researches of those who have devoted time and energy to the questions at issue.

Constitutions cannot, in the Abbé Sieyès manner, be evolved out of the inner consciousness of learned professors. They cannot be left to be invented by imaginative minds, nor do they come into existence automatically. In modern times every new constitution must be evolved by a process of careful selection—not indeed of principles but of devices. The principles, admittedly, are not matters in which there can be much room for choice. They are determined by the historical evolution of the country concerned. These principles, interpreted and stated in terms of the tendencies of history and of the necessities of existing political facts arising therefrom, can alone provide the foundation on which constitutions can be built. The selection of devices, however, cannot be left to the moment of controversy or discussion, but should be the result of careful prior study.

Suitable political institutions to meet the requirements of a country cannot be clearly thought out at a time of controversy or crisis. The circumstances which conduce to the birth of a new state or lead to the formulation of a new constitution may be created by blood and iron, but the constitution itself must be planned by careful forethought. The mechanism of a state has to be scientifically wrought and delicately balanced; its parts must dovetail into each other, and it must reflect the fundamental factors of the national life. The attainment of such an equipoise cannot be left to haphazard formulas evolved on the spur of the moment. The exercise of forethought is specially necessary in the case of India, where there are many problems of magnitude to solve and the issues involved are of vital importance. Besides, it is generally agreed that the change in the constitution should come by peaceful transformation and not by violent change. The necessity for the detailed analysis of the different aspects of the problem is therefore all the greater.

In the following pages an attempt has been made to study one important aspect of Indian constitutional problems, namely the interplay of the centripetal and centrifugal forces of Indian politics and the methods of their reconciliation.

The history of India is in one sense the history of the interplay of these forces. Important empires came into existence with powerful centralised governments which held together the diverse elements of the sub-continent, only to crumble into pieces again. At least from the time of the Maurya Empire (320 B.C.) this has been the case. In other countries the states did not fall, but were only supplanted. In India, on the other hand, once the central authority weakened, and thereby the cohesive force of the Empire became impaired, the constituent elements became independent and separate political units. When the Mauryan dynasty became weak it was not supplanted by another; instead, the empire itself disappeared and its component parts became independent kingdoms. Again the centralising forces appeared, established empires, governments and administrations, and the same story was repeated. When the Mogul Empire was no longer governed with vigour, it was not a successful adventurer who deposed the phantom Emperor of Delhi and founded a new dynasty; instead, every local ruler and every provincial governor set himself up as an independent monarch. And yet in the eighteenth century there was in the country a very strong feeling of unity because the spell of the Imperial Throne at Delhi bound every one from the Himalayas to Cape Comorin.

The main problem of the constitution of India, therefore, is to provide a stable equilibrium for its centripetal and centrifugal forces. In India, as we have seen, the centrifugal forces have always been stronger and have ultimately won in the struggle against the central government. This fact argues that any Indian constitution must possess two fundamental attributes. First, the central authority must have sufficient power to hold together the subordinate administrations, and the exercise of its power must continually tend to create the feeling of national loyalty. Secondly, it is necessary that the required autonomy of the subordinate administrations is not infringed in local matters. The central authority must necessarily be created by common consent; but the constitution must essentially provide for the distribution of power between the institutions at the centre and between the centre and its periphery, and for co-ordinating their respective activities. What matters in India is this distribution and co-ordination. The proper distribution of powers between the central authority and the local authorities would alone ensure the permanence of the constitution.

It follows that two dangers must be avoided. First, the erection of the central government into a unitary government. If all powers were vested in the central government a strong state would come into being for a time, but it would not last, as the forces of localism would continually undermine it. The States of India are not 'interpolated passages' in its national history. They represent the inherent particularism of India. A central government which took no account of the states would ignore this most persistent fact of India's history. If in the interests of theoretical uniformity such a course were to be pursued, national life would be endangered and India might be thrown into a state of chaos and anarchy, such as followed the collapse of Mogul rule.

The second danger to be avoided is the assignment of inadequate authority to the central government. Equally great would be the menace that would follow if the central government were not strong enough within its sphere of responsibility to enforce its decisions or to check the forces of disintegration. The first was the mistake of the Hohenstaufens, who ruined the magnificent heritage of Charlemagne and Otho the Great by their fight against the claim of regional autonomy. The second was the mistake which converted the inheritance of Charles V into a phantom empire in which—at least after the Treaty of Westphalia—the sovereign power gravitated from the head to the members of the body politic.

The history of the Holy Roman Empire in its later stages is illuminating and a lesson to all interested in the political evolution of India.

Frederick II, the great Hohenstaufen, had himself by the two pragmatic sanctions dated 1220 and 1232 given the nobles and cities practical sovereignty. The interregnum that followed his death and the disintegration of the Hohenstaufen hegemony strengthened the sovereign rights of the Princes. When Rudolf of Habsburg was elected Emperor the power of the central government was hardly sufficient to keep down even the minor nobility. But by the prestige of the imperial name, and by the persistence which characterised their Royal House, the Habsburgs laid the foundation of another revival of central authority. The Empire became practically hereditary in the House of Austria. From the time of the Golden Bull in 1356 to the Wars of Religion, the Empire continued to grow as a Germanic monarchy.

But even during those days some effort was made to safeguard the position of the *me*-sovereignties. The Bundestag and the Hanseatic Leagues were successful efforts in this direction. The Electors of the Empire formed a union—the Kurfurstenverein—at Binigin in 1424 A.D., and in 1495 A.D. the Imperial Court of Justice was established. Further, the Reichsregiment was formed with a view to protecting the Princes from the autocratic pretensions of the Emperor.

Under Maximilian and Charles V these efforts did not meet with much success. The overwhelming power of Charles V, who as King of Spain, heir to the Duke of Burgundy, master of the hereditary dominions of the Habsburgs, and German Emperor, ruled over territories larger than those which Napoleon ever had under effective control, made the German princes weak. But, in the Wars of Religion that followed, the Electors and Princes asserted themselves. This tendency found its culmination in the Treaty of Westphalia, by which the independence of the constituent states was fully recognised. The Justinian absolutism which the Emperors had tried to develop had failed, and Hippolytus à Lapide denounced the *pseudo-Romanism* of the German Empire, giving to the claims of the Princes a theoretical authority which, in the hands of the great French cardinals, was found to be irresistible. These views gained currency, and the electoral states pressed them with effect at Osnabrück and Münster to safeguard their own independence. The Treaty of Westphalia recognised the sovereignty and independence of the constituent states, and thus put an end to the Emperor's direct rule over those areas which were not his hereditary possessions. No direct interference was henceforth possible in the affairs of the states. All matters of common concern were to be decided by the Diet, which consisted of the Envoys of the Electors, Princes and the Free Cities of the Empire. The subjects which the Diet alone had the right to deal with included:

1. Making war and peace for the Empire.
2. Levying of contributions.
3. Making of common laws.

The peculiarity of the Empire as reconstituted was that it had no common treasury, no proper imperial courts; no system of common defence, since the quota system could not be enforced, and there was no method prescribed for the punishment of a refractory member.

From the Treaty of Westphalia to the formal abolition of the Holy Roman Empire, the Electors and Princes owed only a nominal allegiance to the Emperor. The power was effectively transferred from the head to the members of the Empire. Each principality and electorate set up as a petty kingdom. Prussia soon assumed the dignity of kingship and Germany from that time till its reunification under Bismarck was hardly even a geographical unit. The nominal head of the Empire was powerful only because of his hereditary possessions, and when, as happened in 1742, the imperial Crown passed out of the hands of the Habsburgs, the title itself became a mockery; indeed, Charles VII was elected at the dictation of a French marshal and lived as a pensioner of Louis XV. An effort was made by Joseph II to renovate the decayed machinery of the Empire, but that medieval and Catholic instrument was only put more out of gear by the rude handling of the atheist philosopher King, imbued with the ideas of the French encyclopedists. When Francis II abdicated, the throne of Augustus, Charlemagne, Otho and

Frederick Hohenstaufen was officially relegated to the museum of history, its splendour having already departed with the Treaty of Westphalia.

The Congress of Vienna passed the Act of Foundation of the Germanic Confederation, which, however, was nothing more than the ghost of the Holy Roman Empire haunting its accustomed home.

The constitution of the Germanic Confederation is remarkable for three things:

1. The constituent members were completely free and independent. Though the Diet had a shadowy authority in foreign affairs, all the major states pursued their own policy without any reference to imperial interests.

2. The Confederation had no means of giving effect to its own decisions. There was no common army, and the methods of federal execution, tried for the first and last time in the Schleswig-Holstein question, led to war between Austria and Prussia.

3. There was no authority in the Confederation to decide either matters affecting Germany as a whole or those affecting the internal affairs of the states. In fact all the states had become fully sovereign, the Electors having taken the title of Kings. The Confederation

was established (1) to meet the vague demand, voiced all over Germany, for a visible symbol of unity, and (2) because Metternich thought that it would provide him with an instrument to control the affairs of the minor Princes, anxious as he was to establish Austrian hegemony in Central Europe.

The history of the German (Holy Roman) Empire and of the Confederation of Germany is full of valuable lessons for those interested in the future of India. It provides the example of a great country dissolving into petty states by the operation of forces many of which are present in the India of today. The centrifugal tendency inherent in autonomous groups received full play in Germany with every measure which weakened the central government. The Princes of Germany, as are the Princes of India, were sovereigns in their own right. There was no joint machinery for making laws or for enforcing decisions. This is the case in India. So long as the central authority was strong, as under the Hohenstaufens or under Charles V, the Princes bowed before the dictates of the Emperor. The states in India today submit to the exercise of an authority they cannot resist. But unless, by their consent, effective machinery be created in time which shall guarantee their rights, while it reserves necessary powers to a common central government, the future of India may not be bright. The fight between the centripetal and centrifugal forces (witness the claim of the Nehru Report to control the Princes: and the claim of the Princes that their relations are with the British Crown) must be ended, and this can only be achieved by balancing the forces in a suitable constitution.

The German people had a racial and linguistic unity which the Indian people lack. Germany had a united government for many centuries. But in spite of these advantages its unity broke down. It gave way under the pressure of the disruptive sentiments which naturally developed in regional administrations. The main reason of the collapse was that while the central government was powerful it omitted to provide any institutions which could nourish the national sentiment, or any machinery to focus opinion on matters of common concern. If there had been in Germany a federal court, a federal army, a federal customs union and a federal law-making body, the fall of the imperial government would not have meant the disruption of the Empire. But, because such institutions had not been developed, the authority of the Princes asserted itself in the long run, and Germany disappeared from the map for 200 years, to emerge as a strongly centralised federal government.

The history of the United States is in one sense a commentary on the dissolution of the Holy Roman Empire. The thirteen states which united to establish the Government of the United States were originally independent; but the 150 years that have passed since Washington was elected President have been remarkable mainly for the growth of the federal institutions. These have created national unity where formerly reigned the spirit of local isolation. How this change came about is examined in some detail in Chapter III.

It is sufficient to say here that this development was due, first to the increase of the power of the federal executive resulting from the control of the army, foreign policy, currency and customs; secondly, to the growth of federal institutions, especially the Supreme Court, the Senate and the Chamber; and thirdly, to the wide measure of internal autonomy reserved to the states in matters which were not of common concern. The states have remained independent in those spheres in which their sovereignty was not surrendered, but the seedling of the central government has by careful nursing grown into a massive *banyan* tree under the shade of which the states feel themselves safe from encroachment. The powers of the central government have by the operation of economic and national forces, by judicial decisions, etc., been so aggrandised that one penetrating writer described the political organism of the United States as a congressional government. In India the tendency towards the aggrandisement of the central power has operated not only with much greater vigour but with an entire want of discrimination. The result is that the states which negotiated on terms of equality with the Company have been forced to accept a paramountcy which is incredibly wide. This phenomenon led one distinguished Viceroy to state publicly that the rights of the states were derived from the Crown and that the Crown had voluntarily set limits on its own authority. Though this untenable theory has now been abandoned, it is sufficiently indicative of the extraordinary increase in the authority of the central government which has been the dominant fact in the political evolution of India during the last one hundred years.

The division of central and local power in the federal constitutions of the self-governing Dominions also reveals two important facts. The position in Australia fundamentally differs from the position in Canada. A full analysis of this difference is made in Chapter IV. The first important point for our present purpose is that though in these countries there were no forces of historical particularism fighting for the maintenance of sovereign authority, yet it was realised that the development of local institutions and the strict limitation of central authority were not merely necessary but fundamental. Secondly, it is remarkable that an alteration of the respective powers of the central and local governments can only be effected by special methods: in Australia by a referendum; in Canada by a change in the British North America Act. The change is not left at the discretion of the central legislature, of which the power is strictly limited.

Nowhere else was the reconciliation between the claims of local "sovereignty" and the demands of the central government so satisfactorily effected as in the German Reich founded by Bismarck. Where Austria, in spite of Kaunitz, Thugun, Cobnezel, had signally failed, Bismarck succeeded to a remarkable degree. The demand of the Kings and Princes of Germany for independent existence was met without weakening in any measure the central authority of the Reich. It recognised local sovereignties by leaving the member-states intact with their own institutions, councils and governments, and only certain defined powers were transferred to the central government. But the powers transferred were, in the hands of Prussia, sufficiently large to give the necessary strength to the central government.*

Our attempt is to throw light only on one aspect of the Indian political problem—the relations between British India and the autonomous states under Indian rulers. The purpose of any Indian constitution should be to secure within *a well-defined range* an effective national government consistent with the preservation of the internal autonomy of the sovereign states. These states are not parts of British India. Their inherent rights are guaranteed to them by treaties with the British

* See Appendix II, The German Constitution.

Crown. It is therefore not as a concession to their dynastic and state particularism that a full reservation of their rights should be made in the constitution. Such reservation is necessary because the territories administered by the rulers have full freedom to remain outside a national Indian State unless they can be persuaded to come in voluntarily. The states are therefore entitled to insist upon adequate guarantees for the preservation of all their rights except those that must be assigned to the national government to make it effective. The rights of the states are therefore a governing factor in the solution of the Indian problem.

What is the nature of the autonomy that the Princes claim in regard to their states? It is the right to govern, to control their internal administration without any interference from outside. In matters of common concern it goes without saying they will take no action individually.

It will be seen on analysis that there are two factors which constitute the problem of internal autonomy, one limiting the other—namely, the interests of the common central government and the freedom of administration in local affairs. It is the equilibrium of these forces that we call the constitution. Where there are sovereign bodies possessing inherent sovereign rights the central government can only exercise such powers as are expressly granted to it. The problem is to determine these powers with strict regard to the peculiar conditions of India and to devise institutions for the exercise of these powers which would not override the reserved powers of the constituent states.

This brings us to the question of juridical and judicial guarantees as known to the American Constitution and to that of federal institutions such as the Supreme Court and the Senate. The American Constitution provides juridical guarantees for the sovereignty of the states; the Supreme Court safeguards this, and the Senate embodies the national sovereignty as the complex of the sovereignty of the states. In old Germany the existence of sovereigns, the maintenance by them of separate armies in times of peace, and numerous other symbols of sovereignty, necessarily limited the authority of the central government, and these limitations had to be reflected in the constitution.

An attempt is made in the following pages to discuss the nature and form of the guarantees which would satisfy the legitimate demands of the Indian States. An attempt is also made to examine the nature and variety of functions which the states would have to surrender if an effective national government is to be created.

Briefly, the Princes would require:

1. The acceptance by the Dominion Government of India of the subsisting treaties as fully binding.

2. The creation of a Supreme Court which would have the right to declare illegal and *ultra vires* any executive or legislative measure which goes against the clauses of a treaty.

3. The creation of an executive body in which the states would have effective representation to decide matters of common concern.

With these safeguards the states would no doubt surrender to the central government the right of exclusive control over matters of common concern.

What are the matters of common concern? In Chapter IV. an attempt is made to examine the list of subjects which have been declared in other federal countries to be within the exclusive jurisdiction of the central government. A few important considerations with regard to India have also been analysed and stated in

Chapter VI. Generally speaking, it may be said that matters of common concern are those in which a decision by a particular state would affect either the peace, tranquillity or good government of the rest of the federal states, or in respect of which uniformity of design, development and control is essential for national growth.

These suggestions are purely tentative. All that is attempted in this monograph is to exhibit the essential factors, the delicate equipoise of which can alone create a constitution for the whole of India. The study of the conflict of centripetal and centrifugal forces in civilised political communities is analysed here, so that those who are engaged in drafting the constitution of India may have at their disposal the solution which other countries have applied in similar circumstances.

One further general consideration may be noticed here. It is said that in these days of advancing democracy there is no place for Princes and their states, and that all governments must conform to the demands of the national will. An examination of advanced modern states does not appear to afford any justification for the view that local autonomous groups must necessarily merge their identity in larger groups. The fall of the Hohenzollerns and the conversion of the German Empire into the German Republic have not abolished the states in Germany. Bavarian and Saxon particularism seems to be as strong today as it was in the days of the Empire. In Soviet Russia every small community which is ethnically separate is being constituted into an autonomous state. Not only substantive nations like Ukrainia, Georgia, Azerbaijan, Khiva and Bokhara, but smaller groups that had previously lost their national identity, are being revived as states, of course with proper safeguards for the central authority. The conclusion that one is entitled to draw from these facts is that every stable constitution must take note of particularistic communities, and that the success or failure of political development is dependent on institutions designed to provide an equilibrium between the powers of the constituent states and the central government. It may be recalled that the discussions prior to the drafting of the Treaty of Versailles proceeded upon the recognition of this principle and that it underlay the formation of two new sovereign states.

CHAPTER II

FEDERALISM IN INDIA

BROADLY speaking, a constitution serves the following three purposes:

1. The distribution and delimitation of public powers.
2. The maintenance of public rights.
3. The declaration of public obligations.

The distribution of public powers requires the definition of (*a*) the respective spheres of authority of the central and local governments, (*b*) the mode of exercising the authority so divided, and (*c*) the regulation of mutual relations between public institutions charged with authority and between the central and local governments. The maintenance of public rights, in its relation to all citizens under the constitution, involves the guarantee to them of a measure of individual liberty by legal sanction—*e.g.*, by means of the writ of *Habeas Corpus*, the freedom of religious practices, and of the expression of personal views. In relation to the States it involves the assignment to the central government of authority to coerce a recalcitrant state.

In a country like India where the minority interests are varied, important and nervous of their special rights, the legal and constitutional guarantees necessary for their satisfaction have to be incorporated in the constitution. These minority interests may be those of communities like the Mussulmans or of political units like the Indian States. The maintenance of their rights is a matter of constitutional provision. Constitutions, too, are increasingly utilised in modern times for the declaration of the government's obligations in certain matters like primary education.

For the realisation of these objects a written constitution is clearly necessary. Viscount Bryce has said:

> 'Where the centrifugal force is potent and especially where there are reasons to apprehend its further development, the establishment of a rigid constitution may become desirable. . . . Where the existence of distinct groups each desiring some control of its own affairs is fully perceived and duly admitted as a factor in the condition of the community, and where it is desired to give

legal recognition to the fact and to protect other local groups or sub-committees from being overridden by the largest among the groups or by the community as a whole, the creation of a rigid constitution offers a valuable means of securing these objects.'*

All these conditions are present in India. The constitution of India will therefore have to be a detailed document clearly defining the scope, the functions and the powers of each body and of each institution created thereunder. The defects incidental to such a constitution are many and important. For one thing, it involves extreme legalism, because the provision for a judicial decision of constitutional issues gives to a Supreme Court an effective veto and vague revisionary powers. A written constitution is necessarily rigid. Being incapable of expansion, it arrests development and entails forcible change in the constitutional laws instead of alteration by gradual evolution.

The constitution of the United States, which has been the model of most written constitutions, fully illustrates these weaknesses. A detailed

* Bryce: *Studies in History and Jurisprudence.* Essay on Centripetal and Centrifugal Forces, p. 220.

study of the constitutional machinery of the United States is attempted in the next chapter. Here it will be sufficient to point to some of the outstanding difficulties experienced in America during the last 150 years. The constitution had of necessity to leave many things vague. Much that was defined was clothed in eighteenth-century phraseology and was the product of political theories which soon became obsolete. The enthronement of the written word was naturally calculated to breed polemics, and its interpretation was left to a court of law. Constitutional development has therefore depended upon legal casuistry, and on numerous occasions in the recent past the Supreme Court of the United States has blocked the way of legislation universally admitted to be of a benevolent character. In 1895 this Court held Income Tax to be unconstitutional: the result was an elaborate and cumbrous process of amendment of the constitution to give the central government the right to levy this tax. The Court's decisions with regard to the right of owning slaves led to the Civil War, and the intention and purpose of the written constitution were decided not by legal argument but by the sword. Again, as one writer has put it:

> 'Regions the fathers never knew were passing under federal control. The Court was given the impossible task of finding in legal terms which daily grew more outworn, solutions to economic problems which daily grew more subtle. . . . Sometimes it has intoned the obscurities of dead philosophers, at others it has voiced the election returns. . . .'*

In recent times the Court has declared as unconstitutional an Employers' Liability Act, a Workmen's Compensation Act, a Child Labour Act, a Corrupt Practices Act, and a Minimum Wage Act.

As for the Senate, the share which this body, as representing all the states combined, has in appointments, foreign policy, etc., gives to it, in comparison with the Lower House, a far larger measure of power. It is, as a recent writer has put it, 'a gargantuan cabinet for a continent of Rabelaisian diversity.' The Senate when originally constituted consisted only of 26 members, but now contains 96. This enlargement has been automatic as more states have come in, since the constitution provided that each state, whether it be Nevada

* Smellie, *The American Federal System*, p. 141.

with 80,000 inhabitants or New York with 10 millions, should have two members.

Consistently with the strict division of the respective functions and powers of the constituent states and the central government, the constitution also provided for the gradual unification of the states—a process which had achieved enough success to justify President Wilson in remarking that the United States had ceased to be a plural noun. A common citizenship and a single nationality have been developed while the local autonomy of states has been preserved. Moreover, by the legal devices of restriction the centralisation of administrative functions has been prevented; otherwise in such a large geographical area as the United States there would have been 'apoplexy in the centre and anæmia at the circumference.'

So far as British India is concerned a written constitution is inevitable, as it will have to be embodied in an Act of Parliament. So far as the states are concerned this constitution can only come into existence by treaties.* The only question is whether such an Act should be a detailed instrument by which every func-

* See Chapter V.

tion is enumerated and a judicial machinery be established to secure the constitution against legislative encroachments. The special arguments in favour of a judicial machinery in India to preserve the integrity of the constitution are dealt with elsewhere.* In view, however, of the inherent rights of the Indian States and the need for preserving the cultural and religious liberty as well as the political rights of the minorities—both considerations of a fundamental character—the Indian constitution must provide a judicial machinery explicitly vested with the authority to declare *ultra vires* any legislation which infringes the constitution. The difficulties inevitably arising from such a position must be faced: especially the possibility that any law made by the supreme legislature might be declared invalid after it had been on the statute book for years. The creation of a super-legislative body in the form of a union council, or senate, in which the states would be represented *qua* states, is also likely to lead to conflicts with the elected legislature which, modelled on the British Parliament, would be apt to claim the same sovereign authority.

* See Chapter VI.

The ideal of the existing Indian Legislature has been the British House of Commons. The history of the last ten years has shown that any attempt to limit the power of the Lower House is deeply resented by the people of British India. The Council of State, which was created as a revisory body, has practically been unable to assert its authority. The Government, though constitutionally not responsible to the Legislature, has been anxious to placate the Assembly, while its attitude towards the Council of State, except when it needed the support of this body in disregarding the decision of the other, has been one of indifference, strengthened by the knowledge that it could not assert itself. The relative strength which these two bodies have gained provides an illuminating commentary on the text that where there are two legislative bodies the political centre of gravity will very soon shift to one of them. In the United States and in imperial Germany it shifted to the Senate and to the Bundesrat; in England, France, Canada, etc., to the Lower House. Indian politicians, critical of every attempt to create an institution likely to have a conservative outlook, will not readily consent to the establishment of a super-

Parliamentary body in which the representatives of British India and the Indian States sit together to control policies in respect of matters of common concern laid down in a prescribed schedule.

The essential incompatibility of Parliamentary government with federalism, which implies sovereignty in the constituent states, would have to be clearly borne in mind, and the effort of Indian constitution makers would have to be directed to the protection of the states from encroachment by an elected Lower House always claiming sovereignty as being inherent in the vote of the people.

That the constitution of India if it is to include the states will have to be federal in form, is admitted on all hands.

This implies that the central authority would have to be created by agreement between the federating states, each independent of the other, and would exercise only the powers specifically allotted to it by the constitution or those naturally flowing therefrom: all other powers being exercised by the constituent states. It is the maintenance of this line of division that is of the essence of federalism. Therefore a federal system presupposes:

1. The existence of states independent of each other, willing to enter into a compact for the creation of a central government.

2. A written constitution, ' supreme over all other instruments of government,' which shall only be changed according to a process specifically laid down in the constitution itself.

3. The allocation of definite powers to the central government and the provision of machinery to ensure the effective limitation of the powers in all spheres of government—legislation, judicial competence and executive action.

4. The creation of institutions whereby (i) the spirit of the union and (ii) the rights of the states shall be maintained.

5. The existence of judicial power authoritatively to interpret the constitution.

So far as India is concerned it is clear that certain of the most important elements of federalism already exist, though in an inchoate form. There is a central government which exercises the powers necessary for defence, foreign policy and the coercion of recalcitrant states, and it exercises these powers by virtue of their surrender by the Indian States. Thus the activities of the central government in regard to these matters partake of the nature of federal authority, and except in these matters the sovereign authority of the states remains. They enact their own laws and exercise all other powers incidental to their internal sovereignty.

But of course this is federalism only in the embryonic stage, nor does it find expression in any appropriate institutions. The constituent states are not represented in any central body, like the Senate or the Bundesrat, designed to give them as governments the right to share in the determination of common policy. Nor is there any judicial machinery to interpret either the rights of the central government or those of the states. That function is exercised by the Government of India acting as the Paramount Power which professes as a solemn duty the maintenance of the rights of the states. We shall examine later the essential incongruity of such a paramount power umpiring between itself and the Sovereign States with which it is bound by treaties. A further characteristic of the existing position is that although the people of the states are directly affected by the measures of the central authority they have no voice in their determination, and the states themselves deny that the Government of India has any right to associate their peoples with the people of British India.

The apparent exclusion of the states from the central authority imparts to the constitution of the Indian Empire the semblance of a unitary government. The central government, which is also the Government of British India, decides all matters of common concern. The casual observer is thus led to think that British India by its larger size, and therefore as the predominant partner, has the right to decide matters in which the states surrendered their sovereign rights to the Crown. If this view were correct, it would mean a denunciation of the true relationship of the Crown and the states and imply that the present constitution of the Government of India was different from what it is; but this view is quite superficial, based as it is upon mere appearances. The Government of India, so far as it represents the Crown, has never in principle denied the right of the states to express themselves upon questions which concern or affect them. In fact, this right has always been admitted. Indeed, it was to give effect to this admission that the Maharajah of Patiala was nominated a member of the first Legislative Council in 1861, and to the same end of eliciting the point of view of the states there were also nominated from time to time one heir-apparent of a ruler and two Ministers of states who are also state subjects. This direct association with the affairs of British India was not approved of by the Princes themselves, and the Government of India had to revert to the practice of individual negotiation on common questions. Lord Lytton suggested a Privy Council to afford Princes the opportunity of taking a share in shaping the policy of their country. All these attempts were, however, tentative; the constitutional need for developing institutions for the discussion of matters of common concern continued to be increasingly realised, and the idea of meeting it was taken up seriously during the Great War. The 'Chiefs' Conference,' which later on became the Chamber of Princes, and the Standing Committee of the Chamber represent the first cautious steps towards the development of institutions by which the Princes could express their views to the Viceroy in matters which affect them jointly with British India. The success or failure of these institutions is not the point here. What we desire to demonstrate is the fact that the Government of the Crown in India, though unitary in form, is essentially federal in principle.

One great shortcoming of this semi-federal system of government in India, however, is that there is no independent judicial machinery to adjudicate upon inter-statal rights and to prevent the invasion by the central government of the domain of state sovereignty. At the present time all questions of this nature are decided by the Government of India in virtue of its claim of paramountcy. Since all that is regarded by the states as an encroachment on their rights is done in the name of paramountcy the need for competent judicial machinery is insistent, and its creation inseparable alike from justice and the contentment of the states. The states have been asking for a Supreme Court, and the history of the relations between the states and the Government of India during the last seventy years is a conclusive argument in favour of their demand.

The following official statements, which were elicited by the protests of the states, will make the point clear:

'In making its opium arrangements with native states in this Bombay Presidency, the British Government has acted in virtue of its powers as paramount authority and the states were bound to accept its decisions.'

'Upon a full review of the case the Government of India have come to the conclusion that for imperial reasons which apply throughout India . . . it is necessary that . . . Durbar should comply with the wishes of the Government. . . . His Honour must therefore ask the . . . Durbar to carry out the request.'

Every encroachment on the treaty rights of the states has been justified by the Government of India as being implied in the right of paramountcy. This method of the allocation of spheres of power between the central authority and the states, even if there be justification for it in the treaty relations of the two parties, is calculated to retard the growth of an All-India polity. At the same time it has to be remembered that even in the United States the enforcement of constitutional limitations by judicial authority—which now seems so essential and axiomatic—did not come about without bitter and animated controversy. In the very first Congress, Madison argued: 'An exposition of the constitution may come with as much propriety from the legislature as from any other department of Government.'* The executive sternly resisted the attempt of the judiciary to interfere with its functions.† On the other hand, Hamilton (Federalist Essay No. LXXVIII) conclusively demolished this view that either the legislature or the executive has as much right as the Supreme Court to interpret its own powers. He says:

> 'Some perplexity respecting the rights of the courts to pronounce legislative acts void, because contrary to constitution, has arisen from an imagination that the doctrine would imply a superiority of the judiciary to the legislative power. There is no position which depends on clearer principles than that every act of a delegated authority, contrary to the tenor of the commission under which it is exercised, is void. No legislative act contrary to the constitution can therefore be valid. To deny this would be to affirm that the deputy is greater than his

* Quoted in Smellie: *The American Federal System*, p. 139.

† The separation of judicial and executive functions has not yet been secured in British India.

principal: that the servant is above the master: that the representatives of the people are superior to the people themselves. . . . If it be said that the legislative bodies are themselves the constitutional judges of their own powers and that the construction they put upon them is conclusive upon the other departments it may be answered that this cannot be the natural presumption where it is not to be collected from any particular provisions in the constitution.'

The executive as well as Congress, however, held that the right to decide their own powers was left with them and not with the Supreme Court. The power of judicial disallowance came to be accepted fully only after Chief Justice Marshall's famous decision in *Marbury v. Madison* that if the idea of executive or legislative interpretation of powers were accepted 'then written constitutions are absurd attempts to limit a power in its own nature illimitable.'

In the Indian Government of today, as a body representing the whole of India, there is a complete absence of any association between the people of the states and the people of British India. If a federal constitution were to be set up in India this condition would be quite compatible with it. In every system of federation the citizen is subject directly to two authorities—the central federal authority and the state authority. In India, though the central government exercises some measure of indirect authority over the subjects of the states, it exercises no direct authority over them except in the matter of foreign travel. At the same time, though indirect, the authority that the central government does exercise is large and varied, operating almost exclusively through the machinery of the states and under the cover and form of state sovereignty. As there is no direct exercise of authority, the central government is not in any manner responsible to the people of the states. Nor is there any legal or political necessity for creating the government at the centre by the suffrages of these people.

The history of federalism shows that federation has everywhere been the culmination of a union already in being. The fathers of the American Constitution met merely in order to perfect the machinery of the loose confederation which had been organised to fight the colonialism of George III. Germany had all along been a single state divided into autonomous and mutually conflicting units. At no time was the essential unity of the German people destroyed. Even in the period of political decentralisation, between the Treaty of Westphalia and the North German Confederation, the national unity of Germany found a shadowy expression first in the Holy Roman Empire and then in the loose federalism of the constitution of 1815. In the same way during the last 130 years the political unity of India has been practically effected. A federal constitution in India would merely involve the formal ratification of existing conditions, necessarily accompanied by the creation of appropriate institutions.

CHAPTER III

SOME FEDERAL CONSTITUTIONS

THE thirteen colonies which revolted against the mercantilism which characterised the government of George III established amongst themselves a loose confederation in order to secure unity of action. It is not to be supposed that they desired to establish a united government; they merely combined against the common enemy.

The Congress established by the articles of confederation had no authority to legislate for them, nor could it enforce its decisions except through the agency of the state governments. After the war even this very loose confederacy threatened to disappear. If the states were not to fall apart and develop as separate and totally independent republics it was necessary that a more effective union should be devised. There was general agreement that the defects of the confederation should be removed, but the politicians of the states were by no means agreed on the necessity of establishing a powerful Central Government.

The Convention which was called devised a constitution in which the principle of inherent sovereignty of the constituent states was reconciled with the exercise of necessary executive power by a Central Government. The American Constitution is a very short document which has been read aloud in twenty-three minutes. But it laid down the main principles on which the government of the Union was to be based and created the institutions by which those principles were to be carried out.

The United States is, as its name implies, a union of states. The Constitution recognises this fundamental fact and embodies the principle that the Central Government can only exercise those powers which are expressly granted to it. The residuary powers belong to the states. The accepted principles of judicial interpretation of the constitutional powers of the Central Government are (1) that every power so claimed 'should be articulated to some provision of the constitution'; (2) 'where there is such articulation, interpretation should be liberal.' The powers of the Central Government are therefore strictly limited and comprise those expressly granted and those which naturally follow from such.

The Constitution gives exclusive power to the Federal Government in the following matters:

To lay and collect taxes, duties, imposts, and excises, to pay the debts and provide for the common defence and general welfare of the United States, but all duties, imposts, and excises shall be uniform throughout the United States;

To borrow money on the credit of the United States;

To regulate commerce with foreign nations and among the several States, and with the Indian tribes;

To establish an uniform rule of naturalisation, and uniform laws on the subject of bankruptcies throughout the United States;

To coin money, regulate the value thereof, and of foreign coin, and fix the standard of weights and measures;

To provide for the punishment of counterfeiting the securities and current coin of the United States;

To establish post offices and post roads;

To promote the progress of science and useful arts, by securing for limited times to authors and inventors the exclusive rights to their respective writings and discoveries;

To constitute tribunals inferior to the Supreme Court;

To define and punish piracies and felonies committed on the high seas and offences against the law of nations;

To declare war, grant letters of marque and reprisal and make rules concerning captures on the land and water;

To raise and support armies, but no appropriation of money to that use shall be for a longer term than two years;

To provide and maintain a navy;

To make rules for the government and regulation of the land and naval forces;

To provide for calling forth the militia to execute the laws of the Union, suppress insurrections, and repel invasions;

To provide for organising, arming and disciplining the militia, and for governing such part of them as may be employed in the service of the United States, reserving to the States respectively the appointment of the officers and the authority of training the militia according to the discipline prescribed by Congress;

To exercise exclusive legislation in all cases whatsoever, over such district (not exceeding ten miles square) as may, by cession of particular States and the acceptance of Congress, become the seat of the Government of the United States, and to exercise like authority over all places purchased by the consent of the legislature of the State in which the same shall be, for the erection of forts, magazines, arsenals, dockyards, and other needful building; and

To make all laws which shall be necessary and proper for carrying into execution the foregoing powers, and all other powers vested by this Constitution in the Government of the United States, or in any department or officer thereof.

These clauses define the limits of the power of the Federal Government. The 10th Amendment further states expressly that the powers not delegated to the United States by the Constitution nor prohibited by it to the states are reserved to the states respectively or to the people.

Every express provision of powers to the Central Government produces a progeny of its own. Thus the powers of taxing and borrowing money, of regulating commerce and of carrying on war have given to the Federal Government extensive authority not contemplated under the Constitution. The taxing and borrowing powers have enabled the Federal Government to establish a national bank and to authorise it to issue notes. The right to regulate commerce has been interpreted to mean legislation and control of transportation, control of navigable waters and the right to establish a Railway Commission to control inter-statal traffic.

The rights of the states are protected not merely by the limitation of the rights of the Central Government, but by the recognition expressly contained in the 10th Amendment that the residuary powers are with the states. All authority which is not granted to the Central Government or reserved for the people continues to be vested in the states. As a leading authority has stated, the Constitution 'presupposed and recognised the existence of state governments which had very definite functions and far-reaching powers.'* In the spheres allotted to each, both the Central

* Kimball: *The National Government of the U.S.A.*, p. 52.

Government and the states were supreme and their authority absolute.

Whenever a doubt arises as to the sphere of powers the presumption is in favour of the states. State legislation is barred only by express prohibition in the Constitution. Complementarily, for a legislative act of the Congress there must be an express grant of power. Where jurisdiction is concurrent the federal law, however, overrides the state law.

This division of powers as federal, state, concurrent and national naturally gives rise to a conflict of jurisdictions. The preservation of the due authority of each within its own allotted sphere was the main object of the fathers of the Constitution. The popular idea that the Constitution entrusted this responsibility to the Supreme Court is not strictly correct. The power of legal disallowance, however clearly implied, was not expressly granted to this Court, and the issue thus involved occasioned a prolonged controversy. It was finally settled by the decision of the Supreme Court in the celebrated case of *Marbury v. Madison*, when Chief Justice Marshall, the second founder of the American Constitution, stated the law in the following terms:

'The powers of the Legislature are defined and limited; and that those limits may not be mistaken or forgotten, the Constitution is written. To what purpose are powers limited and what purpose is served by committing the Constitution to writing, if the fullest limits may at any time be passed by those intended to be restricted? The Constitution is either a superior paramount law unchangeable by ordinary means or it is on a level with ordinary legislative acts and like any other act is alterable when the Legislature shall please to alter it. If the former part of the alternative be true then a legislative act contrary to the Constitution is not law; if the latter part be true then written constitutions are absurd attempts on the part of the people to limit a power in its own nature illimitable.'

The principle of judicial disallowance is now universally accepted in America, but there are inherent defects in the resulting system. The gravest of these is that when judicial decisions come into conflict with executive opinions there is no sanction by which the decision of the Court can be enforced. In 1801, when Chief Justice Marshall declared that the

Supreme Court had the authority to compel executive officers to perform specific acts, President Jefferson protested. In 1829, when the Supreme Court ordered the state of Georgia to release persons who had been imprisoned under a local statute, President Jackson declared: 'Justice Marshall has pronounced his judgment: let him enforce it if he can.' In the Dred-Scott case the Supreme Court held that the Congress had no power to prevent slavery in the territories. The reply to this was given by Abraham Lincoln when he said: 'If the policy of the Government is to be irrevocably fixed by decisions of the Supreme Court in ordinary litigation between parties . . . the people will have to cease to be their own rulers.' The deadlock created by such obstructions was only solved by a prolonged Civil War.

Another serious defect of the principle of judicial interpretation of constitutional validity is that every issue has to be fought by ordinary litigation as between private parties; questions of principle are 'fought out within a cloud of specific issues and sicklied o'er with the pale cast of legal thought.' As a recent writer on the American Constitution has put it: 'The less true legal innovation may appear, the greater may be the political consequence. The courts may permit an invasion of liberty under cover of the extension of a specific power given by the constitution to the Government.'

Then, again, a law which may have been on the statute book many years may suddenly be declared unconstitutional. Legal enactments are thus rendered precarious.

These defects of the principle of judicial disallowance would be apt to assume in India an exaggerated form. The states possess exclusive rights of administration in their own territories; therefore unless the Central Government, when it differs from a judicial decision, is prepared to coerce a state by force of arms, the deadlock which President Jackson threatened would often arise. Assume that a specific state law is declared invalid as being against the Constitution. The Central Government holds the view that the judicial decision was wrong and the state was within its rights and was in fact exercising a necessary power. Assume, further, that the state authorities defy the judicial decision. How is the Court to enforce its decision, unless the executive authority is prepared to compel the state to execute a decree which that authority itself believes to be wrong?

Again, the people of India are believed to be litigious by temperament. All their legal acumen would be devoted to the purpose of leading the Supreme Court to declare that every law which they disliked infringed some principle of the Constitution. As the Constitution of India would have to guarantee freedom of religious worship, rights of minorities, etc., there would be no law which would not be open to attack from some point or the other. The Mussulman agitation against the Sarda Act provides an example. The power of judicial disallowance might in India restrict legislative authority to such an extent that legislation might become wellnigh impossible unless extensive authority were reserved to the Central Government.

The institutional guarantee given to the American states centres in the Senate, which represents the states, just as the House of Representatives represents the nation. In the Senate each state is represented by two members. Thus there are ninety-six members for the forty-eight states of the Union. As the Senate represents the states it shares on behalf of the states extensive powers with the executive government. A vital share in foreign policy, treaty making, finance and certain very important appointments is secured to the Senate by the Constitution. Thus the Senate is not merely a legislative body, but an executive organ which shares with the President many functions of importance. Originally it was a body of ambassadors from the states who constituted a permanent Cabinet for the President. When there were only thirteen states a Cabinet of twenty-six was not, perhaps, unworkable, but a cabinet of ninety-six is rather cumbrous, and the history of the Senate's exercise of its share of executive power has shown the weaknesses inherent in the system.

The main characteristics of the constitution of the Senate are that:

1. The Senators represent the states.

2. Each state has equal representation.

3. The Senate shares executive power with the President and legislative power with the House of Representatives.

The fact that the Senate represents the states is what makes the Federal Government a union of states. It is in its character as the institution which represents all the states that the Senate shares the control of foreign policy, and the treaty-making power—the essential attributes of the sovereignty of the states. By reserving those powers to the Senate the states preserve their own sovereignty and assert the principle that the Central Government is only a union of states. The ambassadorial character of the Senate and its share of power constitute what may be called the institutional guarantee of the states as distinct from the juridical guarantee of the Constitution and the judicial guarantee of the Supreme Court.

The equality of representation in the Senate is the device by which particular states are prevented from becoming dominant by reason of their population. It is calculated that eighteen of the smaller states (electing thirty-six members) do not together equal New York in population. Thus each state as a state has an equal degree of control in the Central Government.

It is recognised on all hands that the Senate of the United States is a political institution of great weight, wisdom and responsibility. It has given to the states a sense of security and a feeling that in surrendering their sovereignty to a central authority they have surrendered it only to themselves. It has effectively reconciled the doctrine of states' rights with the necessity for a strong Central Government. The possible objections to such an institution in India are many, and they will be discussed in some detail in a later chapter. So far as America itself is concerned, the Senate has been the means of creating a dangerous division of executive responsibility in important matters. It has made secrecy, despatch and finality impossible in the conduct of foreign affairs. Though the geographical position of America has saved it from disasters which might otherwise have resulted from having the foreign policy of a great Commonwealth conducted by ninety-six members, no impartial critic can say that the right of the Senate to share the treaty-making power has not been a source of weakness to the Federal Government.

The federal constitution of America was cemented by the Civil War and has been strengthened by the evolution of 150 years. Neither the perverse brilliance of Coulhon nor the genius of Jefferson Davis was able to effect a permanent breach in it. But it should not be forgotten that in contrast with India the rights of the states in America, though tenaciously held, were artificial and had not been strengthened by centuries of local feeling and by loyalty to particular dynasties. Further, never was the Constitution seriously threatened from outside. These are considerations which undeniably limit the application of the American doctrines and principles to Indian conditions.

The Constitution of Imperial Germany presents more analogies to the student of Indian politics than does that of the United States of America. The problems that faced the statesmen of 1867 and 1871 were (1) the existence of one state—namely, Prussia—predominant alike in military and financial power, in area and in population; (2) the existence of a large number of minor states, each rooted in historical tradition and intensely jealous of its sovereignty; (3) the interlacing of the territories of Prussia with those of other states in such a manner as to bring it into the closest contact with them all; (4) the complete identity of economic interests resulting from fifty years of the Zollverein which Massen had founded in 1818; (5) the resulting necessity of *voluntary* surrender by each state of a part of its sovereignty in order to make a federation possible.

The union of the American states was a union of equal states. The union of Germany was the federation of the smaller states *with Prussia*. Under the American federation each state had equal rights. In the German Empire, Prussia negotiated with each state separately and made concessions, not always liberal (*e.g.*, in the case of Würtemberg), which suited the occasion. The German Constitution is therefore worth special study. By the North German Confederation of 1867 three main organs were created: the Federal presidency, which was given permanently to the King of Prussia, the Federal Council (the Bundesrat), and the Reichstag. The President represented the Bund in all external matters, though his consent was not necessary to *federal legislation* or to federal taxation. As King of Prussia he retained all his authority over Prussia. As President he summoned and dissolved the Reichstag. The important new body created by the North German Confederation was the Federal Council, or the Bundesrat. This was a body like the American Senate created *out* *of the states*, representing the states, but, unlike the American Senate, dependent entirely on the states. It was 'a syndicate of governmental delegates appointed in assigned numbers by the Bund, who voted as *units* representing the assigned vote, on the instruction of their respective governments.'* Unlike the Senate, again, its deliberations were secret, but like the Senate it shared executive authority. Out of the forty-three votes in the Federal Council seventeen were reserved for Prussia and twenty-six were assigned to the other twenty-one states.

The method by which this Confederation was called into being is also of importance. Prussia conducted independent negotiations with the twenty-one states which were to be federated with her, and concluded separate treaties. The validity of the Constitution rested upon these treaties by which the different rulers surrendered a common measure of their powers. The constituent assembly merely ratified the Constitution created by the treaties. In essence, therefore, the North German Confederation was a permanent alliance of twenty-one states with Prussia. The alliance

* Grant Robertson, *Bismarck*, p. 229.

was on the basis of the guarantee to the states of their internal sovereignty coupled with the surrender of definite powers to a central government constituted out of the states.

The German Empire which came into existence in 1871 was merely the extension of the North German Confederation to include the German states south of the Main. It attained completeness by fitting into the framework of the Constitution of 1867 the remaining states of Bavaria, Würtemberg, Baden and Hesse. The method followed was the same as in 1867. When the ministers of these states arrived at Versailles Bismarck negotiated with them individually.

The Federal Council was as much an essential part of the Imperial Constitution as it was of the North German Confederation. It continued to be a syndicate of governments, a secret diplomatic Congress, an imperial Cabinet, and a legislative body all rolled into one. Of the fifty-eight votes, Prussia had seventeen, Bavaria had six, and the rest were divided unequally. Effective power continued to be in the Federal Council, in which also the particularism of the states was emphasised. Prussia was excluded from the

Foreign Relations Committee. Bavaria had a permanent seat on the Fortification and the Army Committees. The right of declaring any but a defensive war was shared by the Federal Council with the Emperor, and authority in all federal matters was really vested in it. The Reichstag, on the other hand, possessed wide legislative powers. In this matter the German federation went much further than the United States. Article IV of the Imperial Constitution enumerates the subjects allotted to the imperial legislature.*

The peculiar feature of the Constitution of Imperial Germany was the predominance of Prussia. The Constitution had three fundamental objects in view. First, that Prussia should not be overridden by any state or group of states; secondly, that the rights of the states should not be interfered with; and thirdly, that the people of Germany should have a common Parliament, which, however, would not have the power to interfere with the reserved authority of the states.

By giving Prussia seventeen votes in the Bundesrat (fourteen being sufficient to veto constitutional changes) the first object was

* See Appendix, pp. 164-6.

served. By concentrating powers in the hands of the Federal Council created out of state governments the rights of the states were guaranteed. By calling into existence a German Parliament elected by universal suffrage from the whole empire a democratic form was given to the popular demand for unification.

Under the Weimar Constitution (1919), the rights of the states have suffered a diminution. Republican Germany is more unitary and centralised. The course of imperial legislation under the Kaisers had materially encroached upon the rights of the states, and the symbols of sovereignty preserved for them, though outwardly impressive, were in fact illusory, except in so far as these rights were institutionalised in the Federal Council. Even the financial initiative of the states was restricted in favour of the Empire.

Under the new Constitution the Federal Council still exists as representing state governments, and the separate existence of states as autonomous, if not as sovereign units, is recognised. But the basis of the constitution has been changed. It is no longer one of alliance between states and rulers. It is now a Constitution based on the will of the German nation. To that extent the rights of the states have ceased to be inherent, for a constituent assembly or a referendum can change the Constitution without the consent of state Governments.

*

CHAPTER IV

SOME FEDERAL CONSTITUTIONS *continued*

DUE to its historical growth and the fact of its guaranteed neutrality, the Constitution of Switzerland presents some remarkable characteristics. In origin the Cantons were individual sovereign bodies, each possessing marked characteristics. Not only linguistically and ethnologically, but even from the point of view of social organisation, aristocratic communities like that of Geneva differed from the peasant democracies of Unterwalden and Schwyz. Their union was quite loose and the confederacy of 1513, even though it lasted as late as the French Revolution, was hardly a federal government in the modern sense. The Helvetic Republic which resulted from the impact of the French Revolutionary ideal—unitary in its political principles—attempted to create a centralised form of government. But no sooner was the strong arm of Napoleon removed than the Cantons fell apart again and the constituent states of a former day asserted their individual sovereignty, practically ignoring the Central Government.

It required a war of secession to bind the states together, and a genuine federal union was established in 1848. As amended in 1878, that Constitution is still the fundamental law of the Swiss state.

The Swiss National Government has only those powers that have been specially conferred upon it by the Constitution. It is expressly laid down that the Cantons are sovereign and retain all sovereign authority which they have not delegated to the Federal Government. The states possess equal rights, unlike the states of Germany. The division of powers follows the principle of legislative centralisation with administrative decentralisation; that is to say, that while the area reserved for federal legislation is much wider than that for state legislation, the federal laws are administered through the Cantonal agency. The federal legislature deals with the regulation of religious bodies, prevention of epidemics, and even such minor details as game laws. On the other hand, the functions of the Federal executive are limited: they are practically confined to foreign affairs, customs administration, posts and telegraphs, alcohol monopoly and social insurance. But the confederation has a sort of supervisory legislative authority over the Cantons. Moreover, by the method of referendum many additional subjects are being brought within the authority of the Federal legislature.

The Central Government of Switzerland may be said in many respects to be the very embodiment of Federalism. As Professor Dicey says:

> 'Everywhere through the Swiss arrangements you may observe a desire to keep a sort of balance between different states. The members of the Council are seven in number; each member must of necessity belong to a different Canton. The Federal Parliament meets at Berne: the federal court sits at Lausanne in the Canton of Vaud: the federal university is allotted to a third Canton, namely Zürich.'*

The federal principle also finds full play in the fundamental institutions. The Senate is comprised of two members from each Canton, while the Federal House, like the Reichstag and the American House of Representatives, is elected to represent the people. The Federal court is charged with the constitu-

* Dicey: *Law of the Constitution*, eighth edition, p. lxxvii.

tional duty of seeing that neither the Cantons nor the confederation trespass upon each other's respective spheres. It has jurisdiction in suits between the confederation and the Cantons and between the Cantons among themselves. The Federal Court performs numerous other duties. For instance, it entertains complaints of the violation of the constitutional rights of citizens, whether cantonal or federal. But it is not empowered to pronounce upon the validity of any federal law. In a small community such as that of Switzerland, where the people may be appealed to by referendum, the need to protect the states from the encroachment of the Federal executive does not arise. It is worthy of notice that in the Swiss confederation, though the Cantons are sovereign and autonomous and the Federal Government possesses only limited powers, yet the institutional and judicial guarantees for the maintenance of state rights are not regarded as very important, nor are they so effective as elsewhere. The Senate, which is constituted out of the states, is a lifeless body. What, then, is the guarantee of the freedom of the states?

The answer to the question lies in the fact

that the Swiss Cantons are not merely the seats of a rooted particularism which the Central Government, however constituted, dare not attack; and they do not suffer from any great inequality of population, wealth or power. In the United States, if the equality of states were not rigidly maintained in the Senate, the predominance of a few states would make the rest dependencies. In the same way, if the other states of Germany were not given weight, they would cease to count in the partnership with Prussia. In Switzerland the location of federal institutions in different Cantons and the individual representation of the Cantons in the Federal Council tend to make the Federal Government itself the champion of states. Besides, it is always possible to appeal to the people themselves by a referendum, and the particularist sentiment is so common to all the Cantons that any tendency to encroach upon the rights of the states is sure to meet with popular disapproval.

The Commonwealth of Australia offers a much more effective solution of federal problems. We are not here concerned with the special features of the Australian Commonwealth as a *Dominion*. These have to do with its relation to the British Crown and its constitution as a parliamentary form of government. We are only concerned with those details of the Australian Constitution which impart to it a federal character.

Australia is essentially a union of states which were individually autonomous before the Commonwealth came into existence. As the preamble of the Commonwealth of Australia Act says: 'Whereas the people of New South Wales, Victoria, South Australia, Queensland and Tasmania . . . have agreed to unite in one indissoluble federal Commonwealth . . . be it therefore enacted.' The preamble gives the clue to the Constitution. The existence of the states as autonomous bodies is assumed, and their union, it is expressly stated, is to be on a federal basis. The unmistakable intention was that the states should continue to enjoy a large measure of internal independence, and that they should not derive their powers from the Federal Government. This, in fact, is the principle which underlies the whole Act. A federal executive, a federal legislature, and a federal court are constituted by the Act, but their powers are defined.

'Every power' (says Sub-section 107, Chapter V) 'of the Parliament of a Colony which has become or becomes a state, shall, unless it is by this constitution exclusively vested in the Parliament of the Commonwealth or withdrawn from the Parliament of the state, continue as at the establishment of the Commonwealth or as at the admission or establishment of the state as the case may be.'

The powers of the Federal Government, though restricted to those expressly granted, are still sufficiently wide. The Federal Parliament has the exclusive right to make laws for the peace, order and good government of the Commonwealth with respect to certain enumerated subjects, chief among them being:

Foreign affairs. Defence. Trade and commerce with other countries and among the states.

Customs. Borrowing on the credit of the Commonwealth. Postal and telegraphic service. Currency coinage and legal tender, naturalisation, etc.

The federal institutions are the Federal Parliament and the Supreme Court. The government of the Commonwealth being parliamentary in character and modelled on the

English Constitution, the authority vested in the Federal Parliament is exercised by the federal executive. This circumstance has naturally tended seriously to affect the position of the states. In Australia, as in other federations, the Senate represents the states and the House represents the nation. The executive authority of the federation is vested in a Cabinet, which in all countries where responsible government prevails becomes entirely dependent on the Lower House. The result is that the institutional representation of the states in a Senate, which is merely a second chamber, and not, like the Senate of the United States, a participant in executive authority, becomes altogether ineffective. The Federal Government does not represent the states as it did in Imperial Germany, or as it does in the United States, but within its sphere it is a body placed above and beyond the states, drawing its authority from the democracy of the Commonwealth. Numerous constitutional devices have been employed to give the Senate a measure of real authority. The scheme of retirement by rotation, the longer term for which the members of the Senate are elected, its immunity from dissolution, etc., are methods by which it was hoped that the Senate would remain an effective political body. Some of these methods have been tried even in the Indian Council of State. But a second chamber can at best be only a revisory chamber, and the essentially democratic first chamber will acquire the authority, financial and other, to enforce its views. Of course the Australian Senate has by no means been the failure that the Indian Council of State has been, but neither has it enjoyed the political importance, authority or dignity of the American Senate, or the Bundesrat.

The Federal Court of the Australian Commonwealth is the authority for judicial interpretation. It can, if the point is raised before it, pass judgment on the validity of both federal and state Acts. This power is not expressly granted to it, but warrant for its exercise is found in the principle of English law that the Courts may declare void any Act of a subordinate legislature which conflicts with the Parliamentary Statute from which that legislature derives its sanction.

The Commonwealth has been in existence only for the last thirty years, and so the process of judicial interpretation has not been in operation for very long. The relations between the states and the Commonwealth are therefore still to a large extent confused and ill-defined, nor have the judicial decisions up to now been wholly consistent with each other.

Again, where in the Commonwealth there is concurrent jurisdiction the federal law supersedes the states' law. Section 109 of the Commonwealth of Australia Act makes this clear. 'When a law of a state is inconsistent with a law of the Commonwealth, the latter shall prevail, and the former shall to the extent of the inconsistency be invalid.'

In interpreting this section Mr. Justice Isaacs laid down:

'Section 109 of the Constitution itself is explicit. The true way to test the argument in the present case is to ask whether the federal Act would be valid supposing the state Act were non-existent. If it would, then in case of inconsistency, the state law, whatever it may be, under whatsoever power enacted, on whatsoever subject, must to the extent of the inconsistency be invalid. This constitutional provision is essential to the very life of the Commonwealth.'*

* Federated Sawmill *v.* James Moore & Son, 1909, 8, C. L. R.

The autonomy of the Australian states, subject as it is to the limitation of the authority surrendered to the central power, and thus withdrawn from the states, is still very extensive. A state can change its own Constitution, subject to the condition that by so doing its Constitution does not clash with the powers and the laws of the central federal authority.

One important provision of the Australian Constitution which is of special interest for India in respect of the future constitutional relationship of the Indian States to the Central Government is that contained in Section 94, which runs as follows:

> 'After five years from the imposition of uniform duties of customs, the Parliament may provide on such basis as it deems fair for the monthly payments to the several states of all surplus revenue of the Commonwealth.'

The prospect of any modern government having surplus revenue is indeed remote, but the equity of this provision is surely undeniable. The revenues accruing to a Central Government undoubtedly belong to the constituent states. The federal authority is empowered to raise them, and after the federal purposes have been fully served the balance should obviously go back to the states. Naturally the question must arise as to what is the minimum expenditure necessary for the Federal Government, and it is not inconceivable that what the Federal Government might regard as its minimum requirement, the states might treat as perhaps extravagant.

In the foregoing paragraphs the main defects of the Australian Constitution have been briefly indicated. It may be repeated that its federal character has been overborne by parliamentary government. As a result of parliamentary responsibility the federal executive has become dependent upon the Lower House, which does not represent the federated states as such, but rather its own electors. The Senate, which was designed to represent the states, has become a second chamber, and thus is unable effectively to influence the policies of the Cabinet. More particularly during the administration of Mr. Hughes, in the later stages of the Great War, federal authority, under the sanction of the Federal Court, received a large extension of power. Thus the lesson which the Australian Constitution unmistakably teaches is that parliamentary government and federalism are in essence incompatible.

The Canadian Constitution is not of much interest to the Indian student who investigates the problem of the rights of the States. Section 9 of the British North America Act (1867) states that—

> ' It shall be lawful for the Queen by and with the advice and consent of the Senate and the House of Commons to make laws . . . in relation to all matters not coming within the classes of subjects assigned exclusively to the Legislatures of the provinces.'

This provision means that the provinces possess only those rights which are expressly granted to them. The cardinal fact of the relations between the British Government in India and the Indian States is that to the states belong all rights which they have not specifically surrendered to that Government either by treaty or valid usage. It is inconceivable that all the states would totally surrender their sovereignty to a Central Government and be content with such enumerated powers as that

Government might think fit to regrant. Thus the Canadian Constitution can offer no help in solving the problem of a federal constitution for India—that is, the construction of British India and the States under a central Federal Government.

The Canadian Constitution is, in fact, a unitary Constitution. Mr. Justice Riddel* has pointed out that in effect the Dominion has the power to veto legislation enacted by a Province within its exclusive sphere. This dictum would appear to result from the fact that the Governor-General has certain powers of disallowing provincial Acts even when they do *not* trench upon federal authority. 'In consequence of parliamentary government, generally speaking the exercise of the Governor-General's prerogative is subject to the advice of federal ministers. Therefore, virtually his veto is the prerogative of the Central Government.' This virtual power, even if rarely exercised, would give to the Central Government effective authority over provincial legislatures. Where this is possible, as in Canada, real federalism does not exist. This is another

* Riddel: *The Canadian Constitution in Form and in Fact.* Columbia University Lectures.

example of a professedly federal Constitution in which, under the stress of parliamentary government, respect for the rights of the states has gone by the board.

Further, it may be noted that formal representation of the states is not enjoined by the Canadian Constitution. The Senate is wholly nominated by the Governor-General, which means in effect by the Central Government. There is neither legislative freedom for the provinces nor institutional guarantees of their authority. Even though under this Constitution there be effective devolution of power in certain limited spheres, yet from the point of view of genuine federation it is by no means a useful model.

CHAPTER V

JURIDICAL GUARANTEES

THE juridical guarantees for the states which enter into a federal union consist in the provisions of the Constitution which reserve to them the rights of undivided sovereignty in all matters which are not either within the exclusive jurisdiction of the central government or withdrawn expressly from the jurisdiction of the states. Thus the Constitution guarantees the existence of the states as sovereign bodies within the Federal State. This, as we have seen, is the case in the United States of America, in Switzerland, in Germany and in Australia. In the Constitutions of Central and South America, which generally follow the model of the United States, the same principle is fully recognised. In Imperial Germany, where the Federal State came into existence as a result of treaties, the juridical guarantee was more effective, in as much as the Constitution thus created by alliances could only be changed by agreement among the states sitting in the Federal Council. In this Council fourteen votes were sufficient to veto any change of an important character. Prussia, having seventeen votes, thus had the right to negative any constitutional amendments. Bavaria, Würtemberg and Saxony in combination had the same power. The Commonwealth of Australia Act, as we have seen, expressly reserves the powers of autonomy to the states constituting the Commonwealth.

So far as India is concerned, the successive Government of India Acts contain the clause that the treaties with the states continue to be binding on the Crown. The Act of 1858 declared:

> All treaties by the said Company shall be binding on Her Majesty; and all contracts, covenants, liabilities and engagements of the said Company made, incurred or entered into before the commencement of this Act, may be enforced by and against the Secretary of State in Council in like manner and in the same courts as they might have been by and against the said Company, if this Act had not been passed.

The Government of India Act (1915) contains the following provision:

> All treaties made by the East India Company, so far as they are in force at the commencement of this Act, are binding on His Majesty, and all contracts made and liabilities incurred by the East India Company may, so far as they are outstanding at the commencement of this Act, be enforced by and against the Secretary of State in Council.

Since the obligation to maintain the treaties and engagements with Indian States inviolable and inviolate is absolute and cannot be either denounced or ignored, it is clear that any new Parliamentary Statute providing for the government of British India is bound to contain the clause that the treaties with the states shall continue to be binding on the Crown and its agents in India. This acceptance by the Crown of the continuously binding character of the treaties and engagements with the states constitutes the guarantee of the sovereign rights of the states.

The federal guarantee would therefore be in the nature of a double insurance. Any Government for the whole of India can only come into being as a result of fresh treaties individually negotiated with the states by a self-governing India. For obviously no Act of Parliament can include the states in an Indian Constitution: still less could the Indian Legislature force the states into a union. So far as British India is concerned, its Constitution can be modified or completely altered by the British Parliament. The demand for Dominion Status is in essence a demand for such an alteration by Parliamentary Statute. But the relationship of the states to the Crown is not subject to alteration by Parliamentary enactments. It can only be changed by the consent of each individual state; in fact, by the alteration of the treaty, engagement or *Sanad* by which the relationship with each particular state is created. It is clear that such a change cannot be brought about by any unilateral Act. To hold the contrary view would be to say that the Crown can legally abolish a state which it is bound by treaty to protect and maintain.

Dominion Status for British India must, therefore, be a result of Parliamentary enactment, and that Parliamentary enactment must of necessity contain a clause providing for the continued observance of the treaties with the Indian States. If this Dominion of British India is to be enlarged so as to include the

Indian States, and thereby to create an Indian Dominion, such a consummation can only be brought about by negotiations with the states and formal treaties contracted with them. By each such treaty a new state would be created to which both British India, however constituted, and the Indian States would voluntarily surrender certain powers to be exclusively exercised by the amalgamated central authority so created. This central authority would no doubt be constituted on a federal basis, and would provide an effective guarantee to the constituent states in the exercise of authority by a system of co-partnership. This subject is dealt with in the next chapter. The point we wish to emphasise here is that any central authority that may be created can only be created by agreement between British India on the one hand, and the states joining the federation on the other. No external power has authority to devise a common Constitution for British India and the states.

The Constitution must therefore assume the existence of the states as sovereigns except in those spheres of government which are allotted to the central authority. Hence the form of government in the constituent states cannot be a matter in which either the central authority or any part of it can possess or legitimately exercise authority. Likewise it is not open to the states to dictate to British India what form of government it should possess; for example, whether British Indian provinces should have merely devolved authority, or whether British India should itself be a federation of provinces. Certain parts of British India are governed under other forms of government than those prevalent in the Governors' provinces; for example, the North-West Frontier Province.

So, also, it is clear that neither a federal Central Government nor British India would be entitled to ask the states to change their traditional forms of government for one which British India might consider to be good. The states would come in as they are, whatever their individual forms of government. It may be that some states would have a constitutional form of government, others a purely personal one. The difference of form need not stand in the way of a federation. In Imperial Germany the free cities like Hamburg and Danzig, with their traditional republican forms of government, freely joined Prussia, Bavaria and other states which were monarchical.

The condition that all the states in a federation should have the same form of government is insisted upon in many federations, notably in the United States of America and in the Union of Soviet Republics. In both these cases there was a compelling motive behind the provision. The United States was anxious to safeguard the republican form of government, and the clause prohibiting the states from departing from this creed was the natural outcome of a fear of monarchy, then almost universally accepted in Europe as the right principle of government. Russia is officially styled the Union of Socialist Soviet Republics. It is clearly stated that the union consists only of Socialist republics organised in the Soviet manner. Naturally, communities organised differently have no place in the Soviet Federation.

If the states entering the Indian Union are to have the right of maintaining their own forms of constitution, it follows that they must possess the right to alter, modify or change those forms. The claim which the Princes now put forward that the Crown is pledged to the maintenance of the existing forms of government in the states would vanish if this principle were accepted. The people of each state would therefore be entitled to demand of their ruler (as even now they are entitled to do) that changes should be introduced in the constitution of the state. The constituent states in the United States of America are entitled to change their constitutions provided the fundamental law of the Federation is not interfered with. The constitution provides that the form of government in all the states shall be republican, and that no differentiation shall be made in suffrage as between negroes and white men. Provided these restrictions are respected, the states are entitled to have any constitution which their people consider to be suitable to them. Thus in some states the women have votes, and the suffrage qualifications are not uniform in all.

Similar is the case in the Australian states. There, of course, the monarchical form of government—the King of England is the Sovereign of each state—could not be changed by a state law. But apart from this fundamental restriction and the necessity of conforming to the federal law in matters which are exclusively within the federal jurisdiction, the states can change their own constitutions. So far as a future federation of India is concerned the same right would clearly belong to the constituent states. There is at present considerable diversity in the constitutions of the states. Within the monarchical framework, Mysore, Travancore, and Cochin have evolved a system of popular government which is entirely effective. In Baroda local government has been strongly developed. A form of government by Council exists in Hyderabad, Indore, Gwalior, Baroda and Kashmir.

From the very denial of the right of the Central Government to insist on a particular form of government for any constituent state, it follows that a constitutional machinery exists in each state by which changes can be effected in the form of its administration. The Butler Committee, in discussing the right of intervention of the Paramount Power, claimed that the Crown could advise the states with regard to constitutional changes in the event of popular agitation. This view is untenable because it invests the Paramount Power with an authority which it has never yet claimed; nor is it reconcilable with the clear provisions of many a treaty or even with valid usage. But the conclusion reached by that Committee brings out two ideas, both of which require consideration. First, no form of government, however guaranteed, can be maintained for all time and continue indefinitely to suit the political needs of a community. This is especially true of India, where education, contact with other civilisations, and freedom and facility of transport are fast transforming the structure of society. Secondly, it is essential that whatever modifications in the existing form of government the changing conditions may require, there should be some machinery through which these modifications could be brought about. The Butler Committee have placed in the Government of India the right to advise the rulers as to changes in their forms of government to suit popular demands. Any Government, or even any individual, may advise any other Government. In Palmerston's time the British Foreign Office used to advise foreign Governments to adopt a limited monarchy with a middle-class Parliament by expatiating on the benefits of such a form of government. Such advice the Political Department is no doubt entitled to give to Indian States. But 'advice' in Indian diplomatic usage is a euphemism, and it does not mean counsel which the party advised may either accept or reject. The Indian States emphatically deny the right of the British Government to require them to change their form of government.

Of course, this does not mean either that the Crown is, or that any future Government of India would be, bound to support by use of force the personal rule of Indian Princes in all circumstances whatever. A constitutional machinery has therefore to be provided which, without eliminating the ruler, will effect the necessary changes to suit the changed circumstances of the country as a whole in strict accord with the material, moral and educational progress of the people of the state.

Such a machinery now exists theoretically in the person of the ruler, who is free to modify or alter the constitution of his government. But human nature being what it is, no ruler can be expected willingly to part with his powers; and unless there is some institution through which the people can effectively express their aspirations, the introduction at the right moment of constitutional changes in the states must remain a doubtful event. On the other hand, the advance of education would create a public opinion within the states and inevitably bring about a change in the form of government. At present popular agitation for constitutional reforms is non-existent in the majority of states. Where education has advanced and agitation already exists it is ineffective, because the people feel that the British Government would intervene to support the ruler. And this is to some extent true.

A drab monotony of constitutional forms is by no means a desirable end in India. The genius of the country has always tended to express itself in wide diversity. There is no reason why for the sake of a theory every part of the country should be forced into a common mould of political organisation. In fact, there is much to be said for a regional diversity of political forms, so long as the principles of good government are observed, and the people are happy and contented and willingly accept the political organisation under which they live. Nor can it be said that the diversity of political organisation will detract from the strength of the Central Government. As long as the entire resources of the community are at the disposal of the Federal Government in times of crisis, no weakness can result from the nature of the internal political organisation of the constituent bodies. On the other hand, it may be that while in British India quick and decisive action may be impossible in a crisis owing to party or parliamentary conventions, in states governed under other forms of government such a difficulty may not arise. To that extent the diversity of forms may be a source of strength to the body politic rather than of weakness.

The basic objections to leaving the states under their own forms of government would appear to be:

First, that the evils inherent in personal government are not eradicated.

Secondly, good government, including the maintenance of fundamental rights, would not be ensured.

These defects could be remedied only by the spread of education and the development of an irresistible public opinion. Against gross oppression, power of intervention could be reserved to the Central Government. A strong public opinion postulates the existence of freedom of association, freedom of speech, the right of criticism in the Press, etc. These, however, are matters of internal government in which the states would normally be supreme. If, therefore, a ruler assumed the powers of dictatorship, suppressed all opinion against himself, and systematically misgoverned the state for his own benefit, there would be no remedy available to the people unless there were an express provision by which the Central Government should be entitled to interpose its authority to set matters right. But if such intervention is not to degenerate into petty and meddling interference it could only be permitted in extreme cases.

The maintenance of a minimum standard of good government in the states in those subjects which are within its own exclusive authority is even more difficult. It would, of course, be possible to include in the constitution a declaration of rights which every state would be normally bound to uphold. But as its executive realisation would rest with the authorities of the states, it might happen that these would remain more a pious ideal than an actuality. This is the case all over the world. An amendment to the constitution of the United States expressly gives the negro the right to vote, but the southern states have so far openly defied or circumvented this law.

The difficulties of ensuring good government in autonomous units are not peculiar to India. The problem exists in a very marked degree in the United States. The United States Government, which may interfere to put down crime in Cuba or Nicaragua, has no authority to do so in Chicago, which is by universal acceptance the metropolis of organised crime. The obvious and gross corruption and misgovernment in many American states constitute a testimony to their persisting sovereignty. Lord Bryce states the problem as follows:

> 'What, then,' the European reader may ask, 'is the National Government without the power and the duty of correcting the social and political evils which it may find to exist in a particular state, and which a vast majority of the nation may condemn? Suppose widespread brigandage to exist in one of the States, endangering life and property. Suppose contracts to be habitually broken, and no redress to be obtainable in State courts. Suppose the police to be in league with assassins. Suppose the most mischievous laws to be enacted. . . . Is the nation obliged to stand by with folded arms,

while it sees a meritorious minority oppressed, the prosperity of the State ruined, a pernicious example set to other States? Is it to be debarred from using its supreme authority to rectify these mischiefs? The answer is "yes." Unless the legislation or administration of such a State transgresses some provision of the Federal constitution, the national government not only ought not to interfere, but cannot interfere. Such a case is not imaginary. . . . In the slave states before the war, although the negroes were not, as a rule, harshly treated, many shocking laws were passed. . . . Even now it sometimes happens that in one or two Western States the roads and even the railways are infested by robbers. There are parts of the country where justice is uncertain. . . . There are districts where armed bands occasionally appear, perpetrating nocturnal outrages which no State police has been provided to check. . . . But the Federal Government looks on unperturbed, with no remorse for neglected duty.'*

Thuggee, masquerading as Klu Klux Klan; mob fury, sublimated by racial fires into lynch

* Bryce, *American Commonwealth*, pp. 337-338.

law; political and municipal corruption as practised by Tammany Hall; organised crimes and murder gangs, extolled by the cinema—all these, before which any misgovernment in Indian States pales into insignificance, have to be tolerated by the Federal Government of the U.S.A. because under the constitution it has not the right to intervene.

The position of the Indian States at the present time is not altogether similar. It stands between the position of Cuba, nominally independent, and the constituent states of America. As the Indian States are 'foreign territory,' like Cuba, the Paramount Power has a right of intervention in case of gross misgovernment. As they are autonomous units, the Government cannot intervene unless certain conditions at present undefined, but well understood, are satisfied. Under a federal system, the powers of intervention of the Central Government would be strictly limited. A vague power of intervention for securing good government would undermine the independence of the states, and it would therefore be necessary to state clearly the conditions which would amount to misgovernment justifying intervention. It is clear that unless the states are completely free within the sphere of their exclusive jurisdiction, they will cease to be sovereignties and will become administrative units.

The position in India is in some ways peculiar. The economic dependence of the states and the fact that most of them are enclaves within the British Indian territory, tangibly subject them to the pressure of British Indian opinion. No barriers can be erected against ideas, and the currents of opinion which flow with such force in British India cannot be diverted so as to leave the states untouched. At the present time the weight of the Government of British India is thrown in the scale against the full realisation of democratic ideals, but when this resistance disappears the overwhelming pressure of British Indian public opinion would make systematic misgovernment and even untrammelled personal rule wellnigh impossible.

The essential thing is not that the monarchical form of government should vanish from the states, but that the absolute personal discretion of the rulers should be tempered with safe and modifying counsel. So long as the subjects of the states enjoy the recognised rights of citizenship, and these rights cannot be overridden by individual caprice; so long as justice is administered without executive interference, and the services are secure and efficient; so long as person, property and honour are safe, industry and agriculture are fostered and education on a large scale is provided, there will be little to cavil at in the government of the states. For the creation of these conditions no particular form of government is indispensable. An autocratic Germany provided all these blessings in a greater degree than any democratic government. But if these essential conditions of the moral and material advancement of a people are not dependent on the forms of government, they must be admitted to be dependent upon the realisation that the State exists for the people.

The problem of the juridical guarantee for the states has therefore two aspects—the unqualified maintenance of the internal sovereignty of the states, and the realisation by the rulers that the guarantee rests upon the assumption that the states exist as purposive organisations to fulfil certain social ideals to which their entire activities shall be devoted.

As far as the rulers are concerned, this guarantee would lay upon them, their heirs and successors, the responsibility to discharge all the obligations of progressive rule. So long as these obligations are discharged their states would remain not merely independent entities, but would have a share in common policy, a position incomparably more beneficial than their isolated existence dating from the time of Lord Hastings. More specifically to the people of the states this guarantee would mean that the administrations of the states would be animated, not by a spirit of private ownership, but by a desire for their progress and well-being. This is the same thing as to say that constitutional government must gradually come into being in the states. This is practical politics; all else is impatient idealism.

From the point of view of British India and of India in general, this guarantee to the states would mean the attainment of a great object at a small price. It cannot be too strongly emphasised that the states are at the present time quasi-independent sovereign units which could not be brought under any constitution without their consent. The particularism of the people of the states and the dynasticism of the rulers are important factors which cannot be brushed aside in any settlement of the all-Indian problem. If, therefore, an all-India constitution is a desideratum—as undoubtedly it is in the view of all thinking men in the Empire—it can only be realised with the willing co-operation of the states. The constitutional guarantee herein suggested is such that while it would not interfere with the powers necessary to a Central Government, it would conserve the internal autonomy of the rulers and subjects of the states, and such preservation is the *sine qua non* of federation within a reasonable time.

It is not assumed that all the states would join such a federation at once. The agreements that would have to be concluded with those states which are willing to do so should be such as to induce the others to join who at first remain outside. They must feel that they stand to gain materially by agreeing to come into an all-India constitution. For those states which elect to remain outside the federation, the *status quo* would have to be maintained and their affairs continue to be regulated by the present arrangements. The constitution would, of course, provide for their entry into the federation at any time.

CHAPTER VI

INSTITUTIONAL GUARANTEES

A FEDERATION of states, as we have already shown, means the creation of a central authority out of the states federated by the surrender of certain powers which originally belonged to the constituent states. As they are not surrendering them to a third party, but to *themselves jointly*, it follows that there should be created certain special institutions in the Central Government which will represent the states and will on their behalf exercise the powers surrendered by them. It is on this basis that the Senates of the United States, Australia, and Switzerland, and the Bundesrat of Imperial Germany were created. They represented the federal principle in the Central Government. The Senate of the United States, as we have already noticed, consists of two members representing each state *qua* state. The same principle is the basis of the constitution of the Senate in Australia and Switzerland. In Imperial Germany the position was more complicated, and the states as substantive sovereignties were represented by their individual governments according to an agreed ratio of representation.

The essential characteristic of these bodies is that they represent the constituent states. In a real federation all matters of common interest should be dealt with by an institution possessing this characteristic. It may be that the states may decide to surrender certain powers in regard to such matters to another body representing the peoples of all the federated states—*e.g.*, the House of Representatives in America. But when the union is between states which differ in resources, population, area and power, such a surrender to an assembly elected on a popular basis would mean the merging of the smaller units in the dominant partner. Thus in India, if the subjects of common concern between British India and the states were to be left exclusively to an Indian Parliament elected on the numerical basis—as all parliaments are bound to be—the result would be a virtual annexation of the states by British India. British India, having four-fifths of the population of India, would have a preponderant majority in an elected Indian Parliament. Decisions by such a Parliament would in effect be the decisions of British India. Where there is no overwhelming difference in area, population and resources between the constituent states, the federal principle may be equally well realised by a Parliament elected on the basis of population. In Switzerland the Senate has but little power, and the concentration of legislative powers in the Parliament may at first sight suggest that the states have no institutional guarantee. But as pointed out in an earlier chapter, the practical equality of population among the cantons and the free use of referendum made such a guarantee unnecessary. The case of Australia is similar. There the existence of Parliamentary government and the natural reluctance of the British people to invest a non-democratic body like the Senate with political authority have operated to undermine its federal character. The result is that under the pressure of Parliamentary government the Australian Senate has lost its power, and the authority of the states is being encroached upon by a central executive responsible to an elected Australian legislature which takes but little notice of state rights.

Clearly, therefore, it is impossible in India to entrust the decision of matters common to

British India and the states to a Parliament representative of the people. Such a proposal would be an invitation to the states to abolish themselves. All matters of common concern must therefore be decided by a Federal Council in which British India and the states are proportionately represented. For purposes of such matters executive authority would have to be shared between the Viceroy's Cabinet and the Federal Council. This is no novel arrangement. There is the example of America, where the Senate, which is constituted out of the states, shares executive power with the President and his Cabinet. This happens especially in the conduct of foreign policy, in matters of defence, and for the purpose of certain important appointments. Such division of authority was even more marked in the Bundesrat of the German Empire. The Federal Council, as representing the states, shared with the Kaiser the duties of the federal executive. It is the German analogy that would be more applicable to the conditions of India.

How, then, is the Federal Council to be constituted? It is obvious that if it is to represent British India and the states, the Council will have to be a fairly large body consisting of (say) 150 members. Of these, 100 would represent British India and 50 would represent the states. Those representing British India would naturally be elected from the central legislature of British India. The representation of the states would, however, present difficulties. If all the 108 states which are at present members of the Chamber of Princes in their own right were to be individually represented, the Council would become an unwieldy body. The feasible course would seem to be to allot permanent seats to such states as are clearly entitled to them by their area, population and revenue. The rest would have to be grouped for purposes of representation in the Federal Council.

It may pertinently be asked how any Federal Council could be formed to include the representation of the 600 odd states, all claiming internal autonomy. It should not be forgotten that a large majority of them are so small that they cannot maintain even the forms of a regular administration. The Right Hon. Srinivasa Sastri pointed out some time ago that if any such federation as is discussed here is to take place, not more than thirty or forty of the states could claim to be included in the federation. At first sight it would seem that the existence of a very large number of petty states renders the idea of federation impracticable. Luckily, however, the geographical position of these states solves the difficulty. The minor states can be grouped together as—

1. The Southern Mahratta States.
2. The Kathiawad (minor) States.
3. The Central Provinces States.
4. The States of Bihar and Orissa.
5. The Simla Hill States.
6. The Bundelkand States.

These could be organised as sub-federations, and thus could be represented in the Federal Council on some intelligible basis.

Sub-federations are not unknown to recent constitutional practice. The U.S.S.R. mainly consists of sub-federations such as that of Trans-Caucasia. The Government of India itself created and maintained for a long time a common organisation which approximated as nearly as anything could to a sub-federation. This was the Rajstanik Court for the Kathiawad States. If the smaller states were organised into sub-federations they would be able not merely to create and maintain judicial and administrative institutions at present beyond their individual resources, but to secure adequate representation in the proposed Federal Council.*

In the Federal Council the representatives of the states need not necessarily be the Ruling Princes themselves, but, of course, if a ruler chose to appoint himself as the state representative there could be no possible objection. The Federal Council would be a permanent institution which it would not be within the power of the Governor-General to dissolve, but he would have the power to prorogue and summon it. This must be so, as the authority of this Council in the spheres that are allotted to it will be co-ordinate with his own. The renewal of its membership so far as British India is concerned would be dependent on the general elections, as those elected to the Council from the Central Legislature would undergo change with every new Chamber. But so far as the states are concerned the personnel of representation would be dependent on their governments. It would be open to a state to recall its representative

* See Appendix I.

and appoint a new one whenever the necessity for replacement arose. This is the procedure followed in the representation of states in the League of Nations. But the member states of the League of Nations have found that a too frequent change of representatives has a detrimental effect on their influence at Geneva. Consequently many states have considered it necessary to appoint permanent delegates, and many others nominate the same representatives year after year. It may be safely assumed that in the proposed Federal Council the Indian States would not change their representatives too frequently.

The suggested Federal Council would focus, by the method of representation outlined, the best political ability of India. The hundred representatives from the Legislature of British India would include men with experience of public affairs, legal and professional training, and high parliamentary gifts. The representatives from the states would bring into the Council men with experience of administration, men who have filled responsible posts in their own governments, diplomatists versed in the handling of delicate state affairs, but withal men thoroughly imbued with the sense of discipline and unlikely to be moved by mere appeals to attractive theories. Such a body would be eminently fitted to be entrusted with executive power. The representatives of British India, being elected from the Central Legislature, would consist predominantly of the supporters of the Government in power, and therefore could not be irresponsible critics. The representatives from the States, being also the nominees of their governments, would approach all proposals from the practical point of view, and so would not constitute an irreconcilable opposition. A Council so composed might well be associated with the Cabinet in the exercise of executive control.

It might be objected that a Federal Council consisting of 150 members would be 'a gargantuan Cabinet'—too large to wield executive authority. This criticism would be legitimate if the Council were to function as a parliamentary body. But much of its work would be of a confidential nature. As such it would require the utmost secrecy, immediate despatch, and close consultation, and the Council would have to adopt the committee system, following the models of the American Senate, the Bundesrat, and the French Chamber.

The American Senate, invested as it is with wide executive power, has to work through Standing Committees. Each Standing Committee is entrusted with the duty of preparing for disposal a special section of the Senate's work. Thus the Standing Finance Committee looks after all matters affecting finance. The most important of these committees is the Foreign Relations Committee. Its president is always a distinguished Senator, who shares with the President the control of Foreign Policy. President Wilson says:

> 'Its [the Senate's] Standing Committees have a very great influence upon the action of the Senate. The Senate is naturally always inclined to listen to their advice, for each committee necessarily knows much more about the subjects assigned to it for consideration than the rest of the Senators can know.'*

The history of President Wilson's own administration provides the most apt illustration of the power of the committees of the Senate. The Peace Treaties of 1919 and the Covenant of the League of Nations, worked out

* Wilson, *The State*, p. 360.

under the personal guidance of the President of the United States, were thrown overboard by the Senate acting on the advice of its Foreign Relations Committee. In a non-parliamentary system, where executive authority is shared between an irremovable President and a Federal Senate representing states, the only workable method of adjusting their relations, if one party is not to become a shadow of the other, is the committee system, since this constantly associates the two in the solution of all problems.

The French committee system, however, differs from the American. In France the government is parliamentary in form. But the existence of numerous groups which unite or fall apart according to the political exigencies of the moment makes the lives of ministries very short. The average life of a French ministry within recent times has been only a few months. If ministries change so frequently, there cannot be any continuity of policy and the affairs of the nation must naturally suffer. The French have got over this difficulty by evolving the committee system. The French Chamber is divided into eleven sections called 'bureaux'* which are equal in size. Every

* *Pourra et Pierre*, vol. v., chapters ii. and iii.

member of the Chamber belongs to one of these committees and pluralism is not permitted. Each of these bureaux elects one or more of its members for the different Standing Committees. The number of members for each committee is decided by the vote of the Chamber. The committees are only nominally elected, as nominations to important committees result from negotiation between political groups, and proportional representation is given to the parties. These committees elect their *rapporteurs*. Though all Bills and Measures have to be submitted to the appropriate committees, the ministers are not entitled to be present. The committees have the right to inspect administrative offices and can call for all papers. The result is that much of the direction and control which nominally vests in the Cabinet is in effect exercised by the committees. In fact, the committees may be said to constitute the real parliamentary government in France, working for a continuity of policy and enforcing systematic control over all administrative departments.

The Bundesrat of the old Imperial German constitution, which shared executive authority in the Federation with the Emperor, also worked through committees. There were eight permanent committees, and it was an absolute rule that at least five of the states should be represented on each committee. These committees were:

1. For land forces and fortifications.
2. For Naval Affairs.

Both these were nominated by the Emperor, and Bavaria, Würtemberg and Saxony were entitled as of right to be represented.

There were also committees:

3. For Tariffs and Taxation.
4. For Trade and Commerce.
5. For Railways, Posts and Telegraphs.
6. For Justice.
7. For Accounts.

These five committees were elected every year by the Bundesrat.

8. The eighth committee was for Foreign Affairs.

On this Prussia was not represented, and the constitution provided that Bavaria, Saxony and Würtemberg should be members of this committee, together with two other states elected by the Bundesrat.

In these committees each member had only one vote. As the governing authority under the old constitution was vested in the Bundesrat, the work of that body in its executive capacity was carried on mainly through these committees.

The Federal Council which has been suggested as the institution to guarantee all the Indian states a share in executive authority over matters of common concern would have to adopt this system of committees. The Standing Committees of the Council, in each of which adequate representation would be given to the Princes, would be for—

1. Defence.
2. Foreign Affairs and Political Relations.
3. Trade and Commerce.
4. Customs and Indirect Taxation.
5. Transport, including Railways.
6. Posts, Telegraphs and Telephones.
7. Currency, Exchange, Banking.

In no case would the representation of the states be less than one-third; and on certain important committees some states, which have special interests, would have to be given a permanent place—*e.g.*, Kashmir on the Committee on Defence, since that state borders on Russia, Chinese Turkestan and on Tibet; Hyderabad on the Committee on Foreign Affairs, since the foreign relations of India would be mainly with Islamic countries. These, however, are questions of detail which would have to be settled in reference to political, historical and other considerations. It may, however, be mentioned that the proposal to confer permanent seats on the Standing Committees is not a novel one. On the Council of the League of Nations the Great Powers have permanent seats allotted to them. Even in Republican Germany, Bavaria is accorded this privilege. Considering the great differences of area, population and revenue among the Indian States, manifestly it would not be fair to treat all of them alike. Important states will not come into any scheme which does not secure to them an effective share in the exercise of the power they surrender.

What are the matters of common concern to be entrusted to the Federal Council? The question is not easy to answer, as the answer must necessarily involve trenching to some extent upon the internal sovereignty of the constituent states. In federal countries the range of subjects on which authority is exclusively given to the Central Government is very wide. In America, for example, foreign policy, defence, control of trade, currency and legal tender, customs, naturalisation, interstatal communications, posts and telegraphs are among the matters of common concern.

In Germany the list is even wider. Besides all the matters mentioned above, the Reich has exclusive legislative authority in such general matters as railroads (except in Bavaria), roads, canals, citizenship, travel, change of residence and carrying on of trades, regulation of weights and measures, patents, copyright, medical and veterinary police. The legislative centralisation in Germany is in striking contrast with its administrative decentralisation.

In Australia the Federal Government has, in addition, exclusive powers of legislation in respect of foreign corporations, trading or financial corporations formed within the limits of the Commonwealth, marriage, divorce and matrimonial causes and parental rights, old age pensions, influx of criminals and industrial disputes.

The foregoing enumerations should be of assistance in determining what should be treated as matters of common concern for the Indian Federal Council. In India, defence, foreign policy, railway and aerial communications, posts and telegraphs, currency and customs have been regarded in the past as matters of common concern, and as such have been decided by the Paramount Power, sometimes on its exclusive authority, sometimes in consultation with the states. As we have noticed before, the exercise of paramount authority, when it was not a mere usurpation, was on the basis of implied or expressed delegation of powers, and therefore the decisions on these subjects have been by an authority constituted for British India and for the states by agreement between the parties. If a common constitution for the whole of India be established, power in regard to these matters would naturally be exercised by the federal authorities. But besides these matters many others now within the exclusive jurisdiction of the states and of British India would have to come within the purview of the common Government—*e.g.*, control of waterways, ports, naturalisation and citizenship, etc.

The following is a tentative list of common subjects:

1. The Defence of India (including Naval, Military and Air Force questions).

Control of state forces during wars, the co-ordination of state forces with federal forces.

2. External relations (including naturalisation of aliens, travel, settlement beyond India).

3. Ports, quarantine regulations, shipping docks, etc.

4. Communications: Railways, tramways, specified trunk roads, interstatal waterways, air routes.

5. Posts, telegraphs, trunk telephones, wireless.

6. Customs and excise.

7. Currency and coinage.

8. Patents, trade marks and copyright.

9. Extradition laws.

10. Control of traffic in arms and ammunition.

11. The right to contract public debt.

These subjects may be analysed under four heads:

1. Security against foreign danger.
2. External relations.
3. Regulation of trade, commerce, etc.
4. Elimination of friction between the constituent states.

The first head includes such subjects as the maintenance of naval, military and aerial forces; the control of strategic lines of railways, airways and naval dockyards; the right to administer certain areas under federal authority; the right to contract public debt, to erect munition factories, to control key industries, etc.

The second head of powers would give to the Federal Government, in co-operation with the British Foreign Office, authority to negotiate treaties, to collaborate in the work of the League of Nations, to regulate foreign commerce, etc.

The third head includes the right to impose All-India customs duties, encourage industries, establish national banks with authority to issue notes, establish scientific and research institutions for the benefit of agriculture and industry, fix railway rates and freights, generally control the alignment and the working of commercial railways, etc.

The fourth head would include matters which, if left to each state, would lead to controversies and conflicts, such as interstatal waterways, patents, copyright, etc.

The surrender of exclusive jurisdiction over

these subjects to a central authority would appear to amount to an encroachment on the sovereignty now possessed by the constituent states of the future. At the present time they undoubtedly possess full jurisdiction over many of these subjects, but over some of them the Government of India exercises direct or indirect control, though the right of decision still belongs to the states. If, therefore, the states were to be persuaded to part with their jurisdiction they would be entitled to insist that they should be adequately represented in the federal authority. They would be entitled to demand that the institutions which would exercise jurisdiction in matters of common concern should be so constituted that important questions of policy would not be decided by the mere weight of numbers. The Federal Council as here proposed preserves the legitimate rights of the states without in any way weakening the central authority created for the whole of India.

The only objection to this proposal, though resulting merely from a democratic fiction rather than from practical statesmanship, would be that it sets up a non-elective body above the British Indian Parliament with wide executive and legislative powers. It would be argued that in matters of common concern it is the British Indian Parliament that should have the final voice. Instead, authority would be vested in a Federal Council which was not directly elected. Thus, it would be said that the scheme strikes at the root of parliamentary government in India.

But this objection possesses but a seeming validity. First, parliamentary government in British India would not be interfered with. British India would have responsible government with representative institutions which would have plenary authority over all matters not reserved for the Central Government. Undoubtedly many matters which are now within the competence of the British Indian Legislature would be placed under the exclusive jurisdiction of the Federal Council—*e.g.*, Customs, railways, etc. But how else is federation to be brought about? The surrender would be common to British India and the states. It must also be remembered that the power now exercised by the British Indian Legislature has been devolved upon it only since the Reforms of 1919.

Further—and this is the important point—

the Federal Council would contain 109 members, elected from the British Indian Central Legislature out of the total of 150. Thus, two-thirds of the Federal Council would be elected representatives of British India, and therefore the objection to the super-Parliamentary character of the Federal Council would seem to be a purely formal one.

It has already been pointed out in a previous chapter that federalism and representative government responsible to an elected legislature cannot go hand in hand. 'Responsible government' means the control of the executive by an elected legislature. If the Federal Executive is made responsible to a body elected on a *non-federal and unitary* basis, then the guarantees provided for the states will become illusory. The representatives of the constituent states might as well not be in the Federal Executive if its life is to be dependent on the vote of the Lower House. The Australian constitution, which attempts to reconcile these two opposing principles, illustrates—as we have already shown—this weakness in a marked degree. The states in Australia have continued to maintain their independence only because there is no 'predominant partner' among them. They are reasonably well balanced as regards size and resources, etc. In India the case is otherwise. In an All-India Parliament constituted on the basis of population, British India would have 80 per cent. of the seats. If a body so constituted were to be vested with sole authority in matters of common concern, the practical result would be a camouflaged annexation of the Indian States. A Parliament under a responsible Government can only be organised on the basis of the Cabinet system and not of the committee system—the Cabinet representing the majority will exercise all the powers nominally given to the Parliament. In a committee system such as would prevail in an institution which directly exercised executive authority the decision would not be solely by numbers, because the committees would be constituted to represent the different interests represented in the Council. Moreover, the recommendations of committees would not be generally by majority vote, but by decisions based on compromise.

A parliamentary government for the *whole* of India is therefore not conceivable if the interests of the states are to be guaranteed and maintained. British India has been promised responsible government. It has also been officially stated that the necessary implication of this promise is Dominion Status. Our proposal is perfectly consistent with the realisation of both these ideals. British India would enjoy responsible government for purposes of its exclusive affairs, and for purposes of All-India affairs, by alliance with the states, a Dominion would come into being, the central authority of which would be created by agreement.

CHAPTER VII

THE FEDERAL COURT

THE division of powers under the proposed constitution between the Central Government and the states and the dual allegiance thereby created necessitate some machinery which should interpret the constitution and enforce the meaning and purpose of the fundamental law. Such a machinery is essential for the citizen in a conflict of jurisdiction between the constituted powers. Both the Central Government and the states have to be guaranteed their rights, which implies that there should be a clear definition of the boundaries of their jurisdiction. Any law which encroaches upon these boundaries would naturally conflict with the reserved jurisdiction of one party or the other and would create a difficulty for the citizen, who is bound to obey it till it is declared to be *ultra vires*. The citizen, in obeying such a law, would render himself liable to punishment under the conflicting laws of the competing authority. Many difficulties of this kind have arisen in the United States.

Lord Bryce, in discussing this dilemma, writes as follows:

'The safe rule for the private citizen may be thus expressed: "Ascertain whether the federal law is constitutional (*i.e.*, such as the Congress has power to pass). If it is, conform your conduct to it at all hazards. If it is not, disregard it." This may seem hard on the private citizen. How shall he settle for himself such a delicate point of law as whether Congress had power to pass a particular statute, seeing that the question may be doubtful and may not have come before courts?'*

It is clear that under a federal system a conflict of laws is inevitable. Whether a particular subject is within the competence of the authority which claims to legislate on it can only be decided by a court. If it is not within the competence of the authority, the attempted legislation is *ipso jure* void. But it can be so declared only by a court. The occasion for pronouncing on the validity of a law may arise either when the executive authority tries to enforce it or when any person pleads it in claiming or defending a

* Bryce, *American Commonwealth*, vol. i., p. 331.

right. The necessity for judicial decision in such cases is clear, as otherwise the rights of the constituent states and of the Central Government would not be safe from encroachment, and the citizen would be called upon to obey conflicting authorities each entitled to his allegiance and each entitled to punish him.

Apart from the conflicts that may arise from the division of sovereignty between the constituent states and the Central Government, there would also be in India the legacy of old claims between the British Government and the Indian States. There are numerous types of cases which have hitherto been decided by the Paramount Power. Similarly as between the states themselves there are cases which are also decided by the Paramount Power in the exercise of the authority given to it by the treaties. The states contend that this procedure is unjust. It is certainly the cause of friction between them and the Government of India. It is urged that when the Paramount Power decides questions arising between the states and British India it is both party and judge, and therefore the states cannot hope to get justice. Even though by its treaties and engagements the Paramount Power in relation to the states stands in a fiduciary position, its identity with the interests of British India is so complete that it is bound to take up a partisan attitude. Besides, the expert opinion which determines the Paramount Power's decisions is that of British Indian officials, whose duty as well as anxiety is to uphold the interests of their particular departments. The legal opinion by which the Government of India is guided in any matter at issue between the states and British India is the opinion of the Law Member of the Governor-General's Council. The opinion on railway matters is the opinion of the Railway Board—a purely British-Indian authority. Thus in every matter of controversy between the Indian States and British India, the scales are weighted against the governments of the Princes.

Moreover, though all such conflicts of interest are justiciable and the questions at issue should be decided according to the principles of law and evidence, the present practice of the Government of India is to issue 'Orders' and 'Decisions' in their executive capacity. As a result, the states are denied the right of argument through counsel; they have not the opportunity to weigh the evidence produced against their claims, which they would have if the cases were decided according to judicial procedure. The fundamental principle of legal procedure is that decisions can only be based on law cited and arguments advanced. It is not open to the court to base its decisions on considerations which are not advanced in open court. But in executive decisions the case is otherwise. In a conflict of interests between the Government of India and the states the decisions of the former are often influenced by considerations extraneous to the merits of the issue involved—such as the financial interests of British India (*e.g.*, in the case of Kathiawad ports), the discrimination in favour of Europeans (*e.g.*, the claim of Kashmir to levy customs duty on postal parcels), etc. In matters of controversy between the states *inter se* the present position is equally unsatisfactory. Executive decisions in such cases are apt to be affected by the personal equation.

With regard to executive decisions of Government departments, Lord Hewart, the Lord Chief Justice of England, has recently written as follows:

'It may well be that in a particular case a perfectly correct opinion may be obtained from some anonymous person, incapable of identification, who heard none of the parties to the controversy, but brought his individual reason to bear in private upon a miscellaneous bundle of correspondence. It is even possible that, in a particular case, a mysterious individual of that kind might not be in the smallest degree tempted or diverted from a sound opinion by the fact, if it happened to be the fact, that he was closely associated with one of the parties to the controversy. But it is manifest that an opinion so arrived at differs by the whole width of the heavens from the decision of a court. The work of a court involves many important ingredients, as for example:

'That the judge is identified and is personally responsible for his decisions.

'That the case, subject to rare exceptions, is conducted in public.

'That the result is governed by the impartial application of principles which are known and established; and

'That all parties to the controversy are fully and fairly heard.'*

* *The New Despotism*, pp. 35-6.

The necessity of a Supreme Court which could adjust not only the conflicts between the Central Government and the states, but also adjudicate in interstatal controversies, is clear. The Princes have been demanding it equally with the people of British India.

Moreover, judicial umpiring on constitutional issues has become of the essence of federalism. Otherwise a written constitution would have no meaning, as Chief Justice Marshall pointed out long ago.* So far as the British political system is concerned this involves no change of procedure. It is true that any statute enacted by Parliament is supreme, and the court cannot question it on the ground of unconstitutionality. But so far as legislative bodies other than the Imperial Parliament are concerned, English constitutional principle assumes the right of courts to decide on the validity or otherwise of their enactments. Thus if the Parliament of Canada enacted a law which directly infringed the provisions of the British North America Act, no court even in Canada would hold it to be valid. The Colonial Laws Validity Act, Section 2, states:

* *Marbury v. Madison.*

'Any Colonial law which is or shall be in any respect repugnant to the provisions of any Act of Parliament extending to the Colony to which such law may relate, or repugnant to any order or regulation made under authority of such Act of Parliament or having in the Colony the force and effect of such Act, shall be read subject to such Act, Order or Regulation, and shall to the extent of such repugnancy, but not otherwise, be and remain absolutely void and inoperative.'

With regard to the powers of Indian Courts to consider whether the legislation of the Governor-General is or is not constitutional, Professor Dicey observes as follows:

'To look at the same thing from another point of view, the courts in India treat the legislation of the Governor-General in a way utterly different from that in which any English Court can treat the Acts of the Imperial Parliament. An Indian tribunal may be called upon to say that an Act passed by the Governor-General need not be obeyed because it is unconstitutional or void.'*

* Dicey, *Law of the Constitution*, p. 98.

The proposal that the Federal Court should be given power to interpret the constitution in order to enforce its provisions does not involve any change from the subsisting practice in India. All it does is to enlarge the sphere of judicial authority. At present the executive decisions of the Paramount Power which infringe the guaranteed rights of a state cannot be adjudicated upon by any municipal court. They are treated as Acts of state.* As these rights would receive the further guarantee of the constitution of India, all acts of the Federal Executive would become subject to the jurisdiction of the Supreme Court and all constitutional rights would be duly protected and permanently enjoyed.

What law will the federal court enforce? Primarily it will enforce the fundamental law which would be the constitution. In enforcing the constitution it will give effect, so far as they apply, to the Federal and the state laws: when these conflict in matters which are common, the federal law will of course prevail, and to that extent the Federal Court will be an organ of the Central Government. Besides this comprehensive power of interpreting the

* *Kamachi Bai v. The Secretary of State.*

constitution and limiting the Central and state Governments to their allotted spheres, the Federal Court will have exclusive jurisdiction in judicial matters affecting the relations with other countries, such as questions of admiralty and maritime jurisdiction; in cases where the Central Government is sued; over subjects which are specifically excluded from the jurisdiction of some states—*e.g.*, the trial of non-state subjects, Europeans, etc., in small and undeveloped areas; and for appeals from areas centrally administered—*e.g.*, Andaman Islands, military cantonments, etc. In speaking of the jurisdiction vested in the Federal Court of the United States, Chancellor Kent says:

> 'All the enumerated cases of Federal cognisance are those which touch the safety, peace and sovereignty of the nation or which presume that State attachments, State prejudices, State jealousies and State interests might sometimes obstruct or control the administration of justice.'*

The Supreme Court in India would have to be vested with similar jurisdiction. It would have to possess such powers, and *only such powers*, as 'touch the safety, peace and sove-

* Kent, *Commentaries*, vol. i., p. 320.

reignty' of India: on the positive side, in respect to relations with other countries and in interstatal controversies; on the negative side for the purpose of eliminating obstruction due to the particularism of the states. Except in these matters the powers of the High Courts of British India and the states would be final. Apart from giving effect to federal law, which, being the law of the land, the state courts will also interpret and enforce, the federal courts will not have concurrent jurisdiction with British Indian or state High Courts. This should be clearly grasped. Chief Justice Marshall says:

> 'The judicial department of every Government is the appropriate organ for construing the legislative acts of that Government. . . . On this principle the construction given by this Court to the constitution and laws of the United States is received by all as the true construction; and on the same principle, the construction given by the Courts of the various States to the legislative acts of those States is received as true unless they come into conflict with the constitution, laws or treaties of the United States.'*

* *Elemendor v. Taylor.*

It would be necessary specially to guard against one misconception. It may be thought that the creation of a court with vague authority to enforce the constitution might lead to attempts by private individuals to utilise the Court for actions against the states. The power of constitutional interpretation is not a general power. It is merely the authority to declare whether a particular law does or does not transgress the limits set to the law-making authority. Such a decision can only be given when the authority of the court is invoked to enforce that law. Therefore this power does not give to the Federal Court the right to entertain suits by private individuals against a state or a ruler alleged to have transgressed legitimate authority. As between the constituent states themselves and between the Central Government and the states, however, the Supreme Court would adjudicate by virtue of its special powers. But action by an individual against a state in an external court would clearly be inconsistent with the sovereignty of that state. This must be rendered impossible by constitutional provision. The American Federal Court did attempt to exercise such authority, and in the well-known case of

Chisholm v. the State of Georgia it was held by that court that the decision of such cases was within its competence. But that decision gave rise to a stormy agitation on the part of the states, and the constitution had to be specially amended to prevent this encroachment by the judiciary on the rights of the states.*

The appointment of the judges of the Federal Court would be a matter of some difficulty. The Viceroy, as representing the King, should have the authority to appoint in consultation with the Standing Committee of Political Relations of the Federal Council, and the Council should have the right to petition the King to veto an appointment. Only in the first instance would all the appointments have to be made at the same time; and on that occasion they would necessarily be the outcome of consultation between the parties to the federation.

Into the selection of judges of the Federal Court no political, party or communal considerations could be allowed to enter; eminent fitness must be the sole criterion. The judges would naturally hold office during good behaviour, and would be removable only by the Viceroy on the resolution of the Federal Coun-

* Eleventh Amendment.

cil carried by a majority of two-thirds of the members present. It is upon the independence of the supreme judiciary, alike from executive control and from party and political pressure, that the British system of government is founded, whether federal or unitary. This independence is a principle which has been tested by many centuries of experience in England. So also in America, in the Dominions and in British India this same principle has formed the basis of government. More than even the parliamentary system, the success of which has at best been partial and by no means universal, the principle of the independence of the judiciary has been found to be the strongest bulwark of the popular rights and the surest safeguard against arbitrary executive action.

In an earlier chapter we have dealt with the weakness of judicial umpiring inherent in a federal system. In a unitary government, such as exists in England, judicial interpretation is a check on administration and not on the sovereignty of Parliament. Therefore its effect is undeniably wholesome. It does not interfere with any law passed by the King in Parliament. The Court, which is the interpreting authority, is only authorised to see that the laws so passed are duly enforced. The judges are not concerned with the morality of the law; their business is to administer the law as it exists. If a decision of the highest court of law brings out a defect, it is for Parliament to alter the law. The courts cannot declare a law to be void because it is defective. The supreme authority of Parliament is universally accepted in English legal theory.

In a federal constitution the vesting in the Supreme Court of the right to interpret the constitution is a denial of the supremacy of the Legislatures. The mere fact that a Legislature has enacted a measure in due form is not conclusive with regard to its validity. The federal court is entitled to declare as null and void any law passed by any authority if it conflicts with the constitution.

It must be stated, however, that the judicial umpiring inseparable from a federal constitution is open to several grave objections. The first and most important is that constitutional developments occur insidiously. They do not result from the conscious exercise of the popular will, but from the exploration of judicial niceties. A harmless-looking decision of an unimportant case may lead to an enlargement of the powers of the Central Government or take away from it authority which is essential to it. A written constitution can only provide a framework. The courts fill up the blank spaces, and this they do, not by any deliberate process, but only incidentally by an interpretation of the law as applicable to the specific cases which come before them. They cannot give weight to political or administrative considerations, as Parliaments can and do when they make laws. Judicial interpretation cannot be guided by any constructive purpose. The result is that the decisions of Courts on constitutional points often give rise to political tendencies wholly against the spirit of the constitution. It was the good fortune of the United States that from its early days to 1835 the federal court was presided over by one of the most eminent judges who ever adorned a Bench—John Marshall (1801-1835). He it was who by his decisions imparted to the constitutional evolution of the United States a remarkable unity of principle and doctrine. It was he who established the very right of the federal court to decide on the validity or otherwise of federal laws. In *Maculloch v. Maryland* he set up the doctrine of 'implied powers.'

It was through his decisions that the supremacy of federal law, when valid, over state constitutions and state laws came to be established. It might easily have been otherwise. If there had not been that continuity or that unity of political principle behind the decisions of the supreme court, the fate of the United States as a federation might easily have been very different. As it was, when the prestige of Marshall's name declined and the tradition which he left behind weakened, the Supreme Court was no longer able to maintain its position as a constitutional umpire. Its decision in *Scott v. Sandford* precipitated the Civil War, and this constitutional deadlock was only solved by resort to arms.

One other difficulty, which would be very serious in India, would arise if either British India or the major states decided to defy the authority of the Supreme Court. In the Cheroke's dispute the State of Georgia did successfully resist the authority of the Supreme Court of the United States. In an Indian Federation, if British India defied the authority of the federal court, there would be no available process for enforcing the Court's decision. In the past this has often happened in the relations between the Government of India and the states. When in Keshab Mahajan's case it was held by the Calcutta High Court that Mayurbhanj was foreign territory, the Government of India, while ostensibly accepting the decision, gained their object in regard to all the Bihar and Orissa States by reducing their status. This they did by the executive act of granting to these states *Sanads*, which materially changed their legal position. Similarly, after the decision in Yusuf Uddin's case, which limited the authority of the Government of India in lands ceded for railway purposes, action was taken by which the legal decision was circumvented. So far as the states are concerned, it is even now impossible for the Government of India to threaten punitive action in every case if its decisions are defied. To use a Viceroy's phrase, the 'mulish obstinacy' of a state might make it difficult for the Government of India to achieve its object, even in small matters, without going to extreme lengths.

Such are the difficulties which will have to be faced. But in so far as the federal judiciary would be the guardian of the rights of the minorities, the federal constitution would be automatically fortified. The British Indian constitution, whatever form it takes, is bound to contain special provisions guaranteeing freedom of religious worship as well as of the cultural and linguistic interests of the minorities. Such provisions would give to the Courts comprehensive power to disallow discriminatory legislation. The Supreme Court would be specially charged with the duty of seeing that legislation by the central authority or by the constituent states did not infringe constitutional guarantees. The extent, degree and range of powers given to the judiciary by these guarantees cannot be anticipated now. They would have to be evolved in course of time as the result of judicial interpretation. A decision (1879) of the Federal Court of the United States, however, illustrates the extent to which such a power may be stretched. Under an ordinance deriving its sanction from a Californian statute, the Sheriff of San Francisco clipped the pigtail of Ho Ahkow, a Chinese prisoner. The Chinaman sued the Sheriff for damages on the ground that the ordinance was in breach of the 14th Amendment, which prohibits the states from making or enforcing any law denying equality of treatment to any person within their jurisdiction. The Federal Court held the ordinance to be invalid on the ground that the pigtail was a matter of religion and honour, and the ordinance by which every person was forced to clip his hair in jail inflicted on the Chinaman special injury.*

The point as it affects India need not be laboured. It is sufficient to emphasise here that, although the disadvantages of a Supreme Court authorised to uphold the constitution or to pronounce upon the validity of laws are many and serious, the countervailing advantages are so great and the political considerations necessitating its creation so important, that those who have to devise a constitutional machinery for India must needs depend upon it for a solution of the problems. It is on the working of this judicial machinery that the success of India's federation would depend. If it either becomes a citadel of social obscurantism, prohibiting progressive legislation on the ground of guarantees to minorities, or of a defiant spirit of advance justifying every legislative action, however fundamentally it may go against the religious and cultural in-

* *Ho Ahkow v. Mathew Nunan* (July, 1879, quoted in Bryce, p. 330).

terest of communities, it will fail to cement the constituent states of the federation. If it becomes a champion of central authority and allows the federal legislature and the executive to override on various pretences the guaranteed rights of the states, or, on the other hand, if it tries to uphold and extend the jurisdiction and sovereignty of the states at the expense of the necessary powers of the Central Government, it will mar the prospects of a free, progressive, and united India. Only if it follows a steady middle course and establishes within a short time a prestige and an ascendancy which neither the Central Government nor the states, neither the majority nor the minority, would dare to question, then, and then only, can India be assured of a safe voyage through the stormy seas of constitutional federation.

CHAPTER VIII

CONCLUSIONS

FROM what has been discussed in the preceding chapters, certain conclusions seem clearly to follow, and they are summarised below:

1. The history of India from the earliest times shows a remarkable persistence of regional particularism. This constant feature finds apt illustration in the existence today of Indian States, which compose more than two-fifths of the country. The annals of various dynasties which rose to paramount power amply testify that it was their attempt to abolish regional autonomy which occasioned the disruption of their respective empires and proved the conception of a united Hindustan to be a chimera. It was their failure to recognise this fissiparous tendency in the body politic of India which caused the breakdown of the Mauraya, the Gupta and the numerous other dynasties, ending with the Moguls, who tried to unite India under a single sovereignty.

2. The history of India makes it equally clear that if the centrifugal forces inherent in

her diversified communities were allowed unrestrained play, the whole country would be split up into little principalities and furnish a parallel to the Balkan States. No central authority would retain a foothold. This deduction is fully borne out by the fate of the Maratha Empire in its last stages. The power acquired by various chieftains — Holkar, Bhonsle, Scindia, Gaekwar and the Southern Jagirdars—reduced to impotence the Central Government, and the enforcement of any uniform policy calculated to preserve the empire was no longer possible.

3. Applying these lessons to the needs of the present day, it is manifestly imperative to avoid both these dangers. The constitution of India should provide for an effective government, constituted on an All-India basis, to deal with matters which affect the country as a whole. The internal autonomy of the sovereign states must be preserved. A centralised unitary government for the whole of India is not yet an attainable ideal. And to leave the Indian States as they are, that is as 'foreign' territories, would be to evade the crux of the problem.

4. A constitution for India which includes

the states obviously cannot be framed by Parliament, because the states are not 'British territory. They can only be brought into the constitutional framework by their free consent. They would naturally be averse from incorporation unless the constitution provided effective guarantees for the maintenance of their identity and of all their rights—the rights which are inherent in their status and are guaranteed but not conferred on them by the subsisting treaties.

5. The most effective constitutional formula which provides guarantees for the sovereignty of the constituent states is Federalism. The essential conditions of Federalism are:

(*a*) That there should be a division of sovereignty among the community—*i.e.*, between the central authority created by the federation and the states which constitute it.

(*b*) That the central authority should have authority only in those matters which are expressly placed within its control.

(*c*) That in all matters which have not been assigned to the central authority the constituent states should be free to exercise full sovereign authority.

(*d*) That this division of powers should be

implemented in the constitution by the institutions created under it; and

(*e*) That the Supreme Judicial authority should be invested with the power to declare *ultra vires* measures which go against the constitution.

6. A federation of British India with the Indian States would present certain features not to be found in any existing federal constitution—*e.g.*:

(*a*) British India, which would be one of the parties to the federation, has twice the combined area of all the states.

(*b*) In resources and population the comparison is even more disproportionate.

There are 108 full-powered states and about 500 others, and no country has yet had to face the problem of federating so many states.

The fact, however, that British India is immeasurably superior in area, resources and population to any state, and indeed to all the states combined, makes it all the more necessary that if federation takes place the guarantee of the rights of the states should be so rigid and inflexible as to render a virtual annexation impossible. The preponderant interest of British India would, of course, have to be safeguarded: but as things are it can be in no danger from the states. The real problem would be to provide against the natural tendency of the big fish to swallow the smaller fish. The practical objection that the states are too numerous and some of them too small to join in a federation is undeniably valid. But of the problem it raises a solution has been suggested—namely, sub-federation. By this means the Bihar and Orissa States can be constituted into one state; the Southern Maratha States into another. The Simla Hill States, the states in the Central Provinces, and the states in Kathiawad, which are not directly represented, can also be similarly treated.

7. To judge from their public pronouncements the constitutional guarantees that the Princes would require before entering a federation would be:

(*a*) Respect for their treaties, which implies recognition of their internal sovereignty, except in so far as it is modified by the constitution of the Federal State.

(*b*) The creation of a federal council to share with the federal executive in the determination, control and execution of policies pertaining to questions of common concern which are assigned to the Central Government.

(*c*) The creation of a Supreme Court—

(1) To enforce the jurisdiction laid down by the constitution.

(2) To adjudicate upon interstatal disputes; and

(3) To deal with cases not within the competence of state Courts—*e.g.*, Admiralty, etc.

8. Respect for the treaties and engagements and the obligations arising thereunder would imply that the present constitutions of the states would be alterable only at their will. The Central Government would not have the authority, which the Government of the United States has, to insist upon any particular form of government.

9. The maintenance of good government in the states and the elimination of the evils of personal misgovernment will be ensured—

(*a*) By the pressure of public opinion.

(*b*) By reserving to the Central Government the right to intervene in well-defined cases, such intervention to be dependent on the assent of a special Standing Committee of the Federal Council.

10. The institutional guarantee which would secure to the princes and states their due share in the control of policy relating to common

subjects would take the form of a federal council in which they would be represented *qua* states to the extent of one-third the total membership. It is suggested that the federal council should be a body of 150 members, of whom 100 would represent British India and 50 would represent the states. The representatives from British India would be elected from its central legislature and would include the Governor-General's Cabinet. The representatives from the states would be nominated by the state Governments or by the sub-federal bodies.

11. The work of the Federal Council would be conducted through Standing Committees established by statute, in some of which certain states would be accorded permanent seats in view of their special importance.

12. The Federal Council would have effective control of all matters of common concern which would be specifically enumerated. Matters of common concern would include defence, foreign policy and imperial relations, railways, posts and telegraph, customs, currency and coinage, etc.

13. The objections to this scheme would probably be that the proposed Federal Council

would be a super-parliamentary body, ultimately not amenable to the control of the electorate: that its creation would be inconsistent with the declaration of 1917, by which British India was promised responsible government: that under the scheme the Parliament of British India would be a subordinate legislative body with only limited authority. These objections can, however, be satisfactorily met.

The Federal Council, as representing the whole of India, would undoubtedly be a super-parliamentary body, but two-thirds of its members would be elected members of the British Indian Legislature. Thus the preponderant voice in the Federal Council would be that of the elected representatives of British India, and therefore from the practical point of view the objection that the Federal Council would be a super-parliamentary body would appear to be invalid.

The argument that the declaration of 1917 promised responsible government and that the scheme here advocated would, if carried out, nullify that declaration is equally insubstantial. The declaration of 1917 referred to the future of British India alone. So far as purely British Indian affairs are concerned, there would be complete responsible government. The British Parliament cannot, even if it desire, establish responsible government for the whole of India, if only because the whole of India is not under British sovereignty. It is, therefore, obvious that in matters which affect the states and British India in common, responsibility of the Central Government to the electorate of British India only is impossible. Our proposal provides parliamentary government for British India in regard to exclusively British Indian matters, and for matters common to British India and the Indian States a scheme of government in which these two parties would unite in due proportion to ensure equitable treatment of each consistently with the advancement of the country as a whole.

14. The third of the guarantees referred to above is that the states would require a Supreme or Federal Court. Without such a judicial authority to give effect to the provisions of the constitution no guarantees, even if contained in the constitution, would have any value. The principle of judicial disallowance of legislation is of the essence of federalism. The states have suffered greatly in the past owing to the absence of judicial machinery to settle the dis-

putes among themselves and between them and the Government of India. But apart from this the maintenance of the rights of the minorities and of other guaranteed interests also demands the establishment of a Supreme Court as the guardian of the constitution.

15. It may be asked, What does British India stand to gain by the suggested concessions to the states ? The answer is that nothing in the nature of a concession has been recommended; what has been recommended is the acceptance of the guarantees which the states must necessarily demand, and which are their due, if it is desired to create a united India. The people of British India have no rights of paramountcy over the states. A self-governing British India with responsible government would have to be content with formal and friendly relations with the neighbouring Indian States. If such a position be deemed satisfactory it would not be necessary to examine our suggestions. If, on the other hand, it be desired to unite India into a single progressive Commonwealth, the two parts of India must be united in one common organisation. Such a common organisation can only result if either British India annexes the states or if it unites with

them on the basis of leaving the states free to exercise those powers which it is not essential for the common Central Government to possess. Clearly there is no question of a concession here.

16. What will be the position of the states if effect is given to the suggestions contained in the previous chapters?

(*a*) The states would have surrendered jurisdiction in certain matters of common interest to a central body in which they are adequately represented. But in relation to existing conditions this proposition does not exhaust the *quid pro quo*. It must be appreciated that:

(1) In many of these matters the Government of India now exercises exclusive authority in so far that it takes action without previous consultation with the States.

(2) Under the federal constitution the states would have a share in the determination and control of policy in all matters assigned to the Central Government.

(*b*) In all other matters complete authority would be reserved to the states, with perfect immunity against legislative or executive encroachment. At present there is no authority to set a limit to the encroachments of the Central Government.

(*c*) In all disputes between states among themselves and between states and British India, and between a state or a group of states and the Government of India, there would be available as of right a judicial machinery which would decide the issues involved on the basis of law and evidence.

(*d*) As the relations between the states and the Government of India would be determined by the terms of the Constitution and by Courts of law, the present wide claims of an uncertain position of paramountcy would *ipso facto* cease to apply.

(*e*) The Central Government would, however, continue to exercise the right of intervention in the following cases, and the following cases only:

(1) If resistance were offered to the enforcement of federal law. This happens even now. [*Vide* the Resolution of the Government of India in the Manipur case.]

(2) If federal property were attacked. This power also is at present exercised by the Government of India. [*Vide* the Mail Robbery Rules.]

(3) If a state were to decline to enforce the judgments of the federal courts.

(4) If gross misgovernment were to occur, assuming that the Committee of political relations of the Federal Council found such misgovernment to exist in fact.

Thus the position of the states would be immune against caprice, co-operation would give place to compulsion, and common matters would be decided by joint authority. The exclusive authority of the states would be guaranteed by the constitution; the very executive organs of the Federal Government, held in check by a supreme judiciary, would provide such a guarantee. There would be freedom and security for the states which would conduce to their development and accelerate their advancement, while to the Central Government would be reserved the rights necessary to safeguard the peace, tranquillity and good government of the whole of India.

APPENDIX I

NOTE ON INTERSTATAL COURTS FOR SPECIFIED REGIONS

THE existence of a large number of states spread over certain well-defined areas creates a special problem of judicial organisation. The states in Bihar and Orissa, in Kathiawad and in the Simla Hills are too small to maintain efficient judicial establishments according to modern standards. Besides, between the states there arise numerous controversies which are proper subjects for judicial decision. It has been suggested in a preceding chapter that a possible solution of this problem might be found in the establishment of common institutions. The Government of India held this view at one time. A Rajsthanik court was established in Kathiawad to which the states surrendered certain classes of cases. Over this court presided a British officer lent by the Government of India. A court of *Vakils* was established for the Rajputana States also. An extension of this principle, by agreement among the states, would seem to be desirable, especially where the states, though politically separate, form a convenient geographical unit.

In this connection the Central American Court of Justice provides a valuable model.

In 1907 five Central American Republics—Costa Rica, Guatemala, Honduras, Nicaragua and Salvador—signed at Washington a convention instituting a Court of Justice, with the object of deciding peacefully all matters of controversy arising between the signatories. The thirteenth article of the Treaty declared that the Central American Court represented the conscience of Central America. The court has jurisdiction over:

1. Cases of all kinds between the signatory states where agreement has not been reached by ordinary diplomatic methods.

2. All cases relating to breaches of treaties, agreements or conventions by a signatory state.

3. Matters referred for opinion by the states.

The jurisdiction of the Court can be enlarged by special Resolutions of the legislatures of the states, giving to the Court additional powers. The Court consists of five judges—one from each state.

When questions are submitted to the Court, the interested party is required to submit a memorandum stating all the points of law and fact relating to the question and the proofs in support of the plea. The Court is required to send this memorandum to the defendant state and to invite its reply within sixty days. This period may be extended at the discretion of the Court. The states may be represented by authorised Agents.

The Court does not possess jurisdiction in suits between private citizens and a state. In the case of *Felipe Lavois v. Honduras*, when the plaintiff, a citizen of Guatemala, brought an action against the defendant state for illegal arrest and deportation, the Court decided that the matter was beyond its competence (December 10, 1913). In another case the Court was asked to declare as null and void the election of Flores by the Congress of Costa Rica, but the Court declared again that the subject fell outside its jurisdiction.

The Central American Court is a purely regional Court, created by agreement between the five signatory states. If a permanent Court of International Justice is established for the two Americas, the Central American Court will, no doubt, still continue to function as a regional organisation.

[For an interesting discussion of the whole subject see Antonio Sanchez de Bustamente, *Cour Permanente de Justice internationale*. Traduit de l'Espagnol par Paul Gonle. Recueil Sirey, Paris, 1925.]

APPENDIX II

THE CONSTITUTION OF THE GERMAN EMPIRE, APRIL 16, 1871

(This translation is based on that in *British and Foreign State Papers*, 1870-1871, but has been slightly modified. The Constitution here printed is that of the German Empire, and was in force from 1871 to 1918.)

CONSTITUTION OF THE GERMAN EMPIRE, BERLIN, APRIL 16, 1871.

HIS Majesty the King of Prussia in the name of the North German Confederation, His Majesty the King of Bavaria, His Majesty the King of Würtemberg, His Royal Highness the Grand Duke of Baden, and His Royal Highness the Grand Duke of Hesse and by Rhine for those parts of the Grand Duchy of Hesse which are south of the river Main, conclude an everlasting Confederation for the protection of the territory of the Confederation and the rights thereof, as well as to care for the welfare of the German people. This Confederation will bear the name 'German Empire,' and is to have the following:

CONSTITUTION

1. Territory of the Confederation.

I. The territory of the Confederation is comprised of the States of Prussia with Lauenburg, Bavaria, Saxony, Würtemberg, Baden, Hesse, Mecklenburg-Schwerin, Saxe-Weimar, Mecklenburg-Strelitz, Oldenburg, Brunswick, Saxe-Meiningen, Saxe-Altenburg, Saxe-Coburg-Gotha, Anhalt, Schwarzburg-Rudolstadt, Schwarzburg-Sondershausen, Waldeck, Reuss Elder Line, Reuss Younger Line, Schaumburg-Lippe, Lippe, Lübeck, Bremen, and Hamburg.

2. Legislature of the Empire.

II. Within this confederate territory the Empire exercises the right of legislation according to the tenour of this Constitution, and with the effect that the Imperial laws take precedence of the laws of the States. The Imperial laws receive their binding power by their publication in the name of the Empire, which takes place by means of an *Imperial Law Gazette*. If the date of its first coming into force is not otherwise fixed in the published law, it comes into force on the fourteenth day after the close of the day on which the part of the *Imperial Law Gazette* which contains it is published at Berlin.

III. For the whole of Germany one common nationality exists, with the effect that every person (subject, State citizen) belonging to any one of the Confederated States is to be treated in every other of the Confederated States as a born native, and accordingly must be permitted to have a fixed dwelling, to trade, to be appointed to public offices, to acquire real estate property, to obtain the rights of a State citizen, and to enjoy all other civil rights under the same presuppositions as the natives, and likewise is to be treated equally with regard to legal prosecution or legal protection.

No German may be restricted from the exercise of this right by the authorities of his own State or by the authorities of any of the other Confederated States.

Those regulations which have reference to the care of the poor and their admission into local parishes are not affected by the principles set down in the first paragraph of this article.

Until further notice the Treaties likewise remain in force which have been entered into by the particular States of the confederation regarding the reception of persons expelled, the care of sick persons, and the burial of deceased persons belonging to the States.

Necessary regulations for military service will be established by means of Imperial legislation.

Every German has the same claim to the protection of the Empire with regard to foreign nations.

IV. The following matters are subject to the superintendence and legislation of the Empire:

1. The regulations as to freedom of translocation, domicile and settlement affairs, right of citizenship, passport and police regulations for strangers, and as to transacting business, including insurance affairs, in so far as these objects are not already provided for by Article III of this Constitution. In regard to Bavaria, however, questions of domicile and settlement, and likewise colonisation and emigration to foreign countries, are excluded herefrom.

2. The customs and commercial legislation and the taxes which are to be applied to the requirements of the Empire.

3. The regulation of the system of coinage, weights and measures, likewise the establishment of principles for the issue of funded and unfunded paper money.

4. The general regulations as to banking.

5. The granting of patents for inventions.

6. The protection of intellectual property.

7. The organisation of the common protection of German commerce in foreign countries, of German vessels and their flags at sea, and the arrangement of a common Consular representation, which is to be salaried by the Empire.

8. Railway affairs—but not in Bavaria except under Article XLVI—and the construction of land and water communications for the defence of the country and for the general intercourse.

9. Navigation and the supervision of rafts on waterways belonging in common to several of the States, and the condition of the waterways, and likewise river or other water dues.

10. Postal and telegraph affairs; in Bavaria and Würtemberg, however, only subject to the provisions of Article LII.

11. Regulations as to the reciprocal execution of judgments in civil affairs and the settlement of requisitions in general.

12. Likewise as to the verification of public documents.

13. The general legislation as to obligatory rights, penal laws, commercial and bill-of-exchange laws, and judicial procedure.

14. The military and naval affairs of the Empire.

15. The measures of medical and veterinary police.

16. The regulations for the press and the right of association.

V. The legislation of the Empire is carried on by the Council of the Confederation and the Imperial Diet (Reichstag). The accordance of the majority of votes in both Assemblies is necessary and sufficient for a law of the Empire.

In projects of law on military affairs, on naval affairs and on the taxes mentioned in Article XXXV, the President has the casting vote in cases where there is a difference of opinion, if his vote is in favour of the maintenance of the existing arrangements.

3. The Council of the Confederation.

VI. The Council of the Confederation consists of the Representatives of the Members of the Confederation, amongst which the votes are divided in such a manner that Prussia has, with the former votes of Hanover, Electoral Hesse, Holstein, Nassau, and Frankfort, seventeen votes, and the rest as follows:

	Votes.
Bavaria	6
Saxony	4
Würtemberg	4
Baden	3
Hesse	3
Mecklenburg-Schwerin	2
Saxe-Weimar	1
Mecklenburg-Strelitz	1
Oldenburg	1
Brunswick	2
Saxe-Meiningen	1
Saxe-Altenburg	1
Saxe-Coburg-Gotha	1
Anhalt	1
Schwarzburg-Rudolstadt	1
Schwarzburg-Sondershausen	1
Waldeck	1
Reuss Elder Line	1
Reuss Younger Line	1
Schaumburg-Lippe	1
Lippe	1
Lübeck	1
Bremen	1
Hamburg	1
Total	58

Each member of the Confederation may nominate as many Plenipotentiaries to the Council of the Confederation as it has votes; but the totality of such votes may only be cast as a unit.

VII. The Council of the Confederation determines:

1. What bills are to be brought before the Imperial Diet, and on the resolutions passed by the same.

2. As to the administrative measures and arrangements necessary for the general execution of the Imperial legislation, in so far as no other Imperial law has decreed to the contrary.

3. As to defects which have made themselves manifest in the execution of the Imperial laws or the above-mentioned measures and arrangements.

Every member of the Confederation has the right to propose bills and to introduce motions, and the Presidency is bound to bring them under debate.

The decisions take place by simple majority, with the reservation of the stipulations in Articles V, XXXVII, and LXXVIII. Non-represented votes or votes without instructions are not counted. In equal divisions the Presidential is the casting vote.

In decisions upon affairs, wherein, according to the rules of this Constitution, the whole Empire has not a common interest, only the votes of those Confederated States are counted which are interested in common.

VIII. The Council of the Confederation forms permanent Committees from its own members:

1. For the land army and fortresses.
2. For naval affairs.
3. For customs and taxes.
4. For commerce and intercourse.
5. For railways, posts and telegraphs.
6. For affairs of justice.
7. For finance.

In each of these Committees, besides the Presidency, at least four of the Confederated States will be represented, and in the same each State has only one vote. In the Committee for the land army and fortresses, Bavaria has a perpetual seat, and the other members thereof as well as the members for the Naval Committee, are nominated by the Emperor; the members of the other Committees are elected by the Council of the Confederation. The composition of these Committees is, to be renewed for every session of the Council of the Confederation or respectively every year, when the outgoing members may be re-elected.

Besides these a Committee for foreign affairs will be formed in the Council of the Confederation, comprised of the representatives of the Kingdoms of Bavaria, Saxony, and Würtemberg, and of two other representatives of the other confederated States who will be yearly elected by the Council of the Confederation, in which Committee Bavaria will preside.

The necessary officials will be placed at the disposal of these Committees.

IX. Every member of the Council of the Confederation has the right to appear in the Imperial Diet, and must at his desire at all times be heard, in order to represent the views of his Government, even when these views have not been adopted by the majority of the Council of the Confederation. No one may at the same time be a member of the Council of the Confederation and of the Imperial Diet.

X. The Emperor is bound to afford the usual diplomatic protection to the members of the Council of the Confederation.

4. The Presidency.

XI. The Presidency of the Confederation belongs to the King of Prussia, who bears the name of German Emperor. The Emperor has to represent the Empire internationally, to declare war and to conclude peace in the name of the Empire, to enter into alliances and other treaties with Foreign Powers, to accredit and to receive Ambassadors.

The consent of the Council of the Confederation is necessary for the declaration of war in the name of the Empire, unless an attack on the territory or the coast of the Confederation has taken place.

In so far as treaties with Foreign States have reference to affairs which, according to Article IV, belong to the jurisdiction of the Imperial Legislature, the consent of the Council of Confederation is requisite for their conclusion, and the sanction of the Imperial Diet for their coming into force.

XII. The Emperor has the right to summon, to open, to prorogue, and to close both the Council of the Confederation and the Imperial Diet.

XIII. The summoning of the Council of the

Confederation, and of the Imperial Diet, takes place once each year, and the Council of the Confederation may be called together for preparation of business without the Imperial Diet being likewise summoned, whereas the latter may not be summoned without the Council of the Confederation.

XIV. The Council of the Confederation must be summoned whenever one-third of the votes require it.

XV. The presidency in the Council of the Confederation and the direction of business belongs to the Chancellor of the Empire, who is to be appointed by the Emperor.

The Chancellor of the Empire may be represented on his giving written information thereof by any other member of the Council of the Confederation.

XVI. The requisite motions, in accordance with the votes of the Council of the Confederation, will be brought before the Imperial Diet in the name of the Emperor, where they will be supported by members of the Council of the Confederation, or by particular commissioners nominated by the latter.

XVII. The formulation and proclamation of the laws of the Empire, and the care of their execution, belongs to the Emperor. The Orders and Decrees of the Emperor are issued in the name of the Empire, and require for their validity the counter-signature of the Chancellor of the Empire, who thereby undertakes the responsibility for them.

XVIII. The Emperor nominates the Imperial officials, receives their oath of allegiance to the Empire, and when necessary decrees their dismissal.

The officials of any State of the Confederation, when appointed to any Imperial office, are entitled to the same rights with respect to the Empire as they would enjoy from their official position in their own State, excepting in such cases as have otherwise been provided for by Imperial legislation before their entrance into the Imperial service.

XIX. Whenever members of the Confederation do not fulfil their Constitutional duties towards the Confederation, they may be constrained to do so by way of execution. Such execution must be decreed by the Council of the Confederation, and be carried out only by the Emperor.

5. Imperial Diet (Reichstag).

XX. The Imperial Diet is elected by universal and direct election with secret votes.

[In addition to the members already allotted to the States comprising the North German Confederation] there are to be elected—in Bavaria, 48; in Würtemberg, 17; in Baden, 14; in Hesse south of the Main, 6 members; and the total number of the members consists, therefore, of 382.

XXI. Officials do not require any leave of absence on entering into the Imperial Diet.

If any member of the Imperial Diet accepts any salaried appointment of the Empire or of any State of the Confederation, or enters into any Imperial or State office to which a higher rank or higher salary is attached, he loses his seat and service in the Diet, and can only regain his position in the same by re-election.

XXII. The proceedings of the Imperial Diet are public.

Accurate reports of the proceedings in the public sittings of the Imperial Diet are privileged [in any court of law].

XXIII. The Imperial Diet has the right to propose laws within the competency of the Empire, and to forward Petitions which have been addressed to it to the Council of the Confederation, or to the Chancellor of the Empire.

XXIV. The legislative period of the Imperial Diet is three years.* For a dissolution of the Imperial Diet within this period a resolution of the Council of the Confederation with the assent of the Emperor is requisite.

XXV. In case of a dissolution of the Imperial Diet, the meetings of the electors must be called within a period of sixty days after such dissolution, and within a period of ninety days the Imperial Diet must be summoned.

XXVI. Without the assent of the Imperial Diet the prorogation of the same may not be extended over thirty days, nor repeated during the same session.

XXVII. The Imperial Diet scrutinises the legality of the credentials of its members and decides thereon. It regulates its own method of business and discipline by a standing order, and elects its President, Vice-Presidents, and Secretaries.

* Amended to five years, March 19, 1888.

XXVIII. The Imperial Diet decides by absolute majority of votes. The presence of a majority of the legal number of members is necessary for the validity of a resolution.

In voting on a matter which, according to the stipulations of this Constitution, is not common to the whole Empire, only the votes of those members will be counted who have been elected in those confederate States to which the matter is common.*

XXIX. The members of the Imperial Diet are representatives of the people as a whole, and are not bound by orders and instructions.

XXX. No member of the Imperial Diet can at any time be proceeded against, either judicially or by way of discipline, on account of his votes, or for expressions made use of in the exercise of his functions, nor can he be made responsible therefor in any way outside the assembly.

XXXI. Without the assent of the Imperial Diet, no member of the same may be placed under examination or arrested during the period of the session for any deed subject to punishment, except when taken in the act or in the course of the following day.

* Repealed by Act of February 24, 1873.

The same assent is needful in arrest for debt.

At the requisition of the Imperial Diet every correctional procedure against a member of the same, and all investigations or civil arrests, must be relinquished for the duration of the period of the session.

XXXII. The members of the Imperial Diet must not receive any salary or indemnification in that capacity.

6. Customs and Commercial Affairs.

XXXIII. Germany forms one customs and commercial territory encircled by a common customs frontier. Those separate parts of territory are excluded which from their position are not adapted for inclusion in the customs frontier.

All articles of free trade in any one of the States of the Confederation may be introduced into any other State of the Confederation, and may only be subjected to a duty in the latter to the extent that similar articles produced in that State are subject to a home duty.

XXXIV. The Hanseatic towns, Bremen and Hamburg, with so much of their own or of the adjacent territory as may be needful for the purpose, remain as free ports outside the common customs frontier until they apply to be admitted therein.

XXXV. The Empire has the sole right of legislation in all Custom House affairs, in the taxation of salt and tobacco produced in the territories of the Confederation, beer and spirit and sugar and syrup or other home productions made from beetroot, in the reciprocal protection against fraud of consumption duties raised in the separate States of the Confederation, as well as in such measures as the Customs Committees may find requisite for the security of the common customs frontier.

In Bavaria, Würtemberg, and Baden, the taxation of the native spirit and beer remains for the present subject to the laws of the land. But the States of the Confederation will direct their efforts to bring about an assimilation in the taxation of these articles likewise.

XXXVI. The collection and administration of the duties and consumption taxes (Article XXXV) remain in the hands of each State of the Confederation, within its own territory, in so far as they have hitherto been so.

The Emperor watches over the observance of the legal procedure through Imperial officials, whom he attaches to the customs or excise offices, and to the directing authorities of the separate States according to the advice of the Committee of the Council of the Confederation for customs and excise affairs.

Information given by these officials as to defects in the execution of the common legislation (Article XXXV) will be laid before the Council of the Confederation for decision.

XXXVII. In decisions relative to the administrative instructions and arrangements (Article XXXV) for the execution of the common legislation, the President has the casting vote, when it is given for the continuance of the existing instruction or arrangement.

XXXVIII. The revenue from the duties mentioned in Article XXXV and from the other taxes mentioned, in so far as they are subject to Imperial legislation, flows into the Imperial Treasury.

This revenue consists of the whole income arising from the duties and other taxes after the deduction of:

1. The tax compensations and abatements according to the laws or the general administrative regulations.

2. The repayments for incorrect levies.

(*a*) For the customs: the expenses which are requisite for the protection and the collection of the duties on that part of the frontiers situated towards foreign countries and in the border district.

(*b*) For the salt tax: the expenses which are incurred for the salaries of the officials who are employed in the salt works to collect and control that tax.

(*c*) For the beet-sugar and tobacco tax: the compensation which, according to the decisions of the Council of the Confederation from time to time, has to be made to the several Federal Governments for the expenses incurred in the administration of these taxes.

(*d*) For the other duties: 15 per cent. of the total income.

The territories situated outside the common customs frontier pay an agreed sum towards defraying the expenses of the Empire.

Bavaria, Würtemberg, and Baden do not participate in the income flowing into the Imperial Treasury from the taxes on spirits and beer, nor in the corresponding part of the above-mentioned agreed payment.

XXXIX. The quarterly summaries which are to be made at the end of each quarter of the year by the collecting authorities of the Federal States, and the final statements to be made at the end of the year and the close of the books of the income from duties and from consumption dues flowing into the Imperial Treasury according to Article XXXVIII, falling due during the quarter or during the financial year, are to be collected into chief summaries, after previous examination, by the directing authorities of the Federal States, and therein each duty is to be separately shown; these summaries are to be sent to the Committee of the Council of the Confederation for financial affairs.

On the basis of these summaries the said Committee will make out provisionally every three months the amount due from the Treasury of each State of the Confederation to the Imperial Treasury, and communicate these amounts to the Council of the Confederation and to the States of the Confederation; it will also present the final statement of these amounts every year, with remarks, to the Council of the Confederation. The Council of the Confederation will decide on the basis of this statement.

XL. The stipulations in the Zollverein Treaty of July 8, 1867, remain in force in so far as they have not been altered by the provisions of this Constitution, and so long as they are not altered in the manner provided in Article VII or Article LXXVIII.

7. Railway Affairs.

XLI. Railways which are considered necessary for the defence of Germany, or for the sake of the common intercourse, may, by virtue of an Imperial law, be constructed on account of the Empire, even against the opposition of the members of the Confederation whose territory is intersected by the railways, but without prejudice to the prerogatives of any State. Concessions to execute the works may also be granted to private contractors, with the right of expropriation.

Every existing railway board of direction is bound to consent to the junction of newly constructed railways at the expense of the same.

The legal enactments which have granted a right of veto to existing railway undertakings against the construction of parallel or competing lines are hereby, without prejudice to rights already gained, repealed for the entire Empire. Nor can such a right of veto be ever granted again in concessions to be issued hereafter.

XLII. The Governments of the Confederation bind themselves to manage the German railways as a uniform network in the interest of the common intercourse, and likewise for this purpose to have all new railways, which are to be made, constructed and fitted up according to uniform rules.

XLIII. For this purpose corresponding working arrangements are to be adopted with all possible dispatch, particularly with regard to railway police regulations. The Empire has likewise to take heed that the railway boards keep the lines at all times in such a state of repair as to ensure safety, and that they provide them with the rolling stock necessary for the traffic.

XLIV. The railway boards are bound to introduce the necessary passenger trains of the proper speed for through traffic, and arrange suitable connections; also the requisite trains to provide for the goods traffic; likewise to arrange direct bookings for passengers and goods traffic, with facilities for changing and conveying goods from one line to the other for the usual payments.

XLV. The Empire exercises control over the tariffs, and will especially operate to the end:

1. That working regulations, in conformity with each other, be introduced as soon as possible on all German railroads.

2. That the greatest possible equalisation and reduction of the tariffs shall take place, and particularly for greater distances an abatement of the tariffs for the transport of coal, coke, timber, ores, stones, salt, raw iron, manures, and similar articles, so as to be more in proportion to the necessities of agriculture and industry, and that the one pfennig tariff may be introduced as speedily as possible.

XLVI. In times of distress, particularly when an unusual dearth of the necessaries of life occurs, the railway boards are bound to introduce temporarily a special lower tariff for the transport of grain, meal, pulse, and potatoes, according to the necessity, as will be determined by the Emperor on the proposal of the respective committee of the Council of the Confederation, which tariff, however, must not be lower than the lowest rate already existing for raw produce on the same line.

The above, as well as the stipulations made

in the Articles XLII to XLV, are not applicable to Bavaria.

But the Empire has the right in regard to Bavaria likewise to lay down, by way of legislation, uniform rules for the construction and fitting up of the railways which are of importance for the defence of the country.

XLVII. The requisitions of the authorities of the Empire relative to making use of the railways for the purpose of the defence of Germany, must be obeyed without question by all the railway boards. In particular, the military and all materials of war are to be conveyed at equally reduced rates.

8. Posts and Telegraphs.

XLVIII. The postal and telegraph affairs will be arranged and administered for the entire German Empire as uniform institutions for State intercourse.

The legislation of the Empire in postal and telegraphic affairs, as provided in Article IV, does not extend to those objects, the regulation of which, according to the principles which govern the North German Postal and Telegraphic Administration, has been left to definitive rules or administrative directions.

XLIX. The revenues of the postal and telegraphic service are pooled for the entire Empire. The expenses will be defrayed from the common revenues; the surplus flow into the Imperial Treasury (Section XII).

L. The chief direction of the postal and telegraphic administration belongs to the Emperor. The officials appointed by him have the duty and the right to take care that uniformity in the organisation of the administration and in carrying on the service, as well as in the qualification of the officials, be introduced and maintained.

The issue of definitive rules and general administrative directions, as well as the sole care of the relations with other postal and telegraphic offices, belongs to the Emperor.

All the officials of the postal and telegraphic administration are bound to obey the Imperial directions. This duty is to be recorded in the oath of service.

The appointment of the requisite principal officials for the administrative authorities of the postal and telegraphic service in the various districts (such as directors, counsellors, chief inspectors), likewise the appointment of the officials acting as the agents of the before-mentioned functionaries, in the service of supervision, etc., in the separate districts (such as inspectors, controllers), proceeds, for the whole territory of the German Empire, from the Emperor, to whom these officials render the oath of service. Timely notice of the appointments in question, for governmental approbation and publication, will be given to the Government of the several States, so far as their territory is thereby concerned.

The other officials necessary for the postal and telegraphic service, as well as all those required for local or technical business, and therefore the officials, etc. acting at the actual place of business, will be appointed by the respective State Governments.

Where there is no independent State post or telegraph administration, the provisions of the special Treaties supply the rule.

LI. In making over the balance of the postal administration for general Imperial purposes (Article XLIX), in consideration of the previous difference in the net incomes obtained by the State postal administrations of the separate territories, the following proceeding is to be observed for the purpose of a corresponding arrangement during the under-mentioned period of transition.

From the postal balances which have accrued in the separate postal districts during the five years 1861 to 1865, an average yearly balance will be calculated, and the share which each separate postal district has had in the postal balance thus shown for the whole territory of the Empire will be fixed according to percentages.

According to the proportion ascertained in this manner, the separate States will be credited for the next eight years after their entrance into the postal administration of the Empire with such quotas as accrue to them from the postal balances produced in the Empire, in account with their other contributions for Imperial purposes.

At the expiration of the eight years all distinctions cease, and the postal balances will flow in undivided account into the Imperial Treasury, according to the principle set forth in Article XLIX.

From the quotas of the postal surplus thus ascertained during the before-mentioned eight years for the Hanseatic towns, one-half will be placed beforehand every year at the disposal of the Emperor, for the purpose, in the first place, of paying therefrom the expenses for the establishment of normal postal institutions in the Hanseatic towns.

LII. The stipulations in the foregoing Articles XLVIII to LI have no application to Bavaria and Würtemberg. In their place the following stipulations are in force for those two States of the Confederation:

To the Empire alone belongs the legislation as to postal and telegraphic privileges, as to the legal relations between both institutions and the public, as to exemptions from postage and rates of postage, excluding, however, the rules and tariff regulations for the domestic circulation of Bavaria and of Würtemberg respectively; likewise under similar reservation the settlement of the fees for telegraphic correspondence.

In the same manner the regulation of the postal and telegraphic intercourse with foreign countries belongs to the Empire, excepting the direct intercourse of Bavaria and of Würtemberg themselves with the neighbouring States which do not belong to the Empire, the regulations as to which remain as stipulated in Article XLIX of the Postal Treaty of November 23, 1867.

Bavaria and Würtemberg do not participate in the income flowing into the Imperial Treasury from the postal and telegraph service.

9. Navy, Shipping and Navigation.

LIII. The navy of the Empire is one united navy under the high command of the Emperor. The organisation and composition thereof is the business of the Emperor, who appoints the naval officers and officials, and into whose service they and the men are to be sworn.

The Harbour of Kiel and that of Jahde are Imperial military harbours.

The necessary expenses for the establishment and maintenance of the war fleet, and the institutions in connection therewith, are paid from the Treasury of the Empire.

The whole of the maritime population of the Empire, including engineers and shipwrights, are free from service in the land army, but, on the other hand, are bound to serve in the Imperial Navy.

The apportionment of recruits is arranged according to the number of the maritime population, and the quota which each State thus contributes is deducted from the contingent to the land army.

LIV. The merchant vessels of all the States of the Confederation form one undivided commercial navy.

The Empire has to determine the method of ascertaining the burthen of sea-going vessels, to grant tonnage certificates, as well as to regulate other ship certificates, and to determine the conditions upon which the permit to command a sea-going vessel depends.

The merchant ships of all the States of the Confederation will be admitted and treated on equal terms in the seaports and in all the natural and artificial waterways of the separate States of the Confederation. The dues to be levied in the seaports from sea-going vessels or their cargoes for using the appliances of navigation must not exceed the expenses which are requisite for the maintenance and ordinary repairs of those appliances.

On all natural waterways dues may only be levied for the use of such appliances as are especially intended for the furtherance of traffic. These dues, as well as the dues payable for making use of such artificial waterways as are State property, must not exceed the expenses which are requisite for the maintenance and ordinary repairs of such erections and works. These regulations are also applicable to rafting so far as it takes place on navigable waterways.

The imposing of other or higher dues on foreign ships, or their cargoes, than those paid by the ships of the Federal States does not belong to any single State, but solely to the Empire.

LV. The flag of the navy and of the mercantile marine is black-white-red.

10. Consular Service.

LVI. The whole of the Consular Service of the German Empire is under the superintendence of the Emperor, who appoints the Consuls after consultation with the Committee of the Council of the Confederation for commerce and traffic.

Within the official district of the Government Consuls no new Consulates for separate States may be erected. The German Consuls exercise the functions of a national Consul for any State of the Confederation not represented in their district. The whole of the existing Consulates for separate States are to be abolished as soon as the organisation of the German Consulates is so completed that the representation of the interests of all the States of the Confederation is recognised by the Council of the Confederation as secured by the German Consulates.

II. MILITARY AFFAIRS OF THE EMPIRE.

LVII. Every German is liable to military service, and cannot have that service performed by substitute.

LVIII. The expenses and burdens of the whole of the military affairs of the Empire are to be borne equally by all of the States of the Confederation and those belonging to them, so that no preferences or overburdening of any single State or class are in principle admissible. Where an equal division of the burdens is not practicable *in natura* without prejudice to the public welfare, the matter is to be arranged on the principles of equity by means of legislation.

LIX. Every German capable of service belongs for seven years to the standing army, as a rule from the completion of the twentieth to the commencement of the twenty-eighth year of his age; that is, for the first three of these years with the colours and for the last four years in the reserve; then for the following five years of his life to the Landwehr. In those States of the Confederation wherein hitherto a longer period than twelve years of service altogether has been legal, the gradual reduction of such service can only take place in so far as regard for the readiness of the Imperial Army for war permits it.

With respect to the emigration of men belonging to the reserve, only those regulations are to be applied which are in force for the emigration of men of the Landwehr.

LX. The effective strength of the German Army in peace is fixed till December 31, 1871, at one per cent. of the population of the year 1867, and the separate States of the Confederation supply it *pro rata.* Subsequently the effective strength of the army in peace will be determined by Imperial legislation.

LXI. After the publication of this Constitution the whole Prussian Military Code of Laws is to be introduced throughout the Empire without delay, both the laws themselves and the regulations, instructions, and rescripts issued for the explanation and completion thereof, especially, therefore, the Military Penal Code of April 3, 1845; the Military Court Martial Regulations of April 3, 1845; the Ordinance upon Courts of Honour of July 20, 1843; the regulations upon recruiting, time of service, allowance and maintenance affairs, billeting, compensations for damages to agriculture, mobilisation, etc., for war and peace. The military Church ritual is, however, excluded.

After the uniform war organisation of the German Army has been effected, a comprehensive military law for the Empire will be laid before the Imperial Diet and the Council of the Confederation for their constitutional decision.

LXII. To cover the outlay necessary for the entire German Army, and the arrangements appertaining thereunto until December 31, 1871, there are yearly to be placed at the disposal of the Emperor as many times 225 thalers (two hundred and twenty-five thalers) as the poll-number of the peace strength of the army amounts to, according to Article LX. (See Section XII.)

After December 31, 1871, these contributions must continue to be paid to the Imperial Treasury by each State of the Confederation. For the calculation thereof the effective strength in peace, as provisionally settled in Article LX, will be taken as the basis until it is altered by an Imperial law.

The expenditure of this sum for the entire Imperial Army and its arrangements will be determined on by the Estimate Law.

In settling the estimates of the military expenses the legal organisation of the Imperial Army, as laid down in this Constitution, will be taken as the basis.

LXIII. The entire land force of the Empire will form a single army, which in war and peace is under the command of the Emperor.

The regiments, etc., will bear consecutive numbers for the entire German Army. For their clothing, the ground colours and fashion of the Royal Prussian Army are to be the model. It is left to the chiefs of the respective contingents to determine the external marks of distinction (cockades, etc.).

It is the duty and the right of the Emperor to take care that all the divisions of troops within the German Army are numerically complete and effective for war, and that unity in the organisation and formation of the armament and command, in the training of the men, as well as in the qualifications of the officers, be established and maintained. For this purpose the Emperor has the right to satisfy himself of the condition of the separate contingents at all times by inspection, and to order the reformation of any defects thereby discovered.

The Emperor determines the effective strength, the division and arrangement of the contingents of the Imperial Army, as well as the organisation of the Landwehr. He also has the right of determining the garrisons within the territories of the Confederation, and to order the embodiment of any part of the Imperial Army in a state of preparation for war.

For the purpose of keeping up the indispensable uniformity in the administration, maintenance, armament, and equipment of all the divisions of troops of the German Army, the orders issued thereon in future for the Prussian Army will be communicated in a suitable manner, through the Committee for the land army and fortresses mentioned in Article VIII, § 1, to the commanders of the other contingents for observance.

LXIV. All German troops are bound to obey the commands of the Emperor unconditionally. This duty is to be specified in the banner-oath.

The Commander-in-Chief of a contingent, likewise all officers who command troops of more than one contingent, and all commanders of fortresses are appointed by the Emperor. The officers appointed by the Emperor take the banner-oath to him. The appointments of Generals and officers acting as Generals within the contingents are at all times subject to the approbation of the Emperor.

The Emperor has the right, for purposes of transfer, with or without promotion, to select, for such appointments as are to be made by him in the Imperial Service, whether in the Prussian Army or in other contingents, from the officers of all the contingents of the Imperial Army.

LXV. The right of erecting fortresses within the territories of the Confederation belongs to the Emperor, who proposes, according to Section XII, the grant of the necessary means for the purpose, in so far as they are not provided for in the ordinary estimates.

LXVI. Where nothing to the contrary is stipulated by particular Conventions, the Sovereigns of the Confederation, or the Senates, appoint the officers of their contingents, subject to the restriction of Article LXIV. They are the chiefs of all the divisions of troops belonging to their territories and enjoy the honours connected therewith. They have especially the right of inspection at all times, and receive, besides the regular reports and announcements of alterations which take place, timely information, for the purpose of Government publication, of all promotions or nominations among the respective divisions of the troops.

Likewise they have the right to make use for purposes of police, not only of their own troops, but also to make requisition for any other division of troops of the Imperial Army which may be located in their territories.

LXVII. Unexpended balances from the military estimate do not belong under any circumstances to a single Government, but at all times to the Imperial Treasury.

LXVIII. The Emperor may, when the public safety is threatened in the territories of the Confederation, declare any part thereof to be in a state of war. Until the promulgation of an Imperial law, which will regulate the premisses, the form of publication and the effects of such a declaration, the rules of the Prussian law of June 4, 1851, remain in force (*Collection of Laws for* 1851, p. 451 and *sqq*.).

*

Final Stipulation to Section 11.

The provisions contained in this section come into force in Bavaria according to the special stipulations of the Treaty of Confederation of November 23, 1870 (*Federal Law Gazette*, 1871, p. 9), under III, Article 5; and in Würtemberg according to the special stipulations of the Military Convention of November 21 to 25, 1870 (*Federal Law Gazette*, 1870, p. 658).

12. Finances of the Empire.

LXIX. All the receipts and disbursements of the Empire must be estimated for each year and be brought into the Imperial estimates. These are to be fixed by a law before the beginning of the financial year, according to the following principles:

LXX. To provide for all common expenses any balances of the preceding year are first of all employed, and likewise the common revenues derived from the duties, the common consumption taxes, and from the postal and telegraph services. In so far as they cannot be provided for by these revenues they are, as long as Imperial taxes are not introduced, to be met by contributions from the single States of the Confederation in proportion to their population, which contributions to the amount estimated in the budget will be assessed by the Chancellor of the Empire.

LXXI. The common disbursements are, as a rule, voted for one year; they may, however, in particular cases, be voted for a longer period.

During the time of transition mentioned in Article LX, the estimates of the expenditure for the army, arranged under heads, are to be laid before the Council of the Confederation and the Imperial Diet only for their information and remembrance.

LXXII. The Chancellor of the Empire is to give account yearly to the Council of the Confederation and to the Imperial Diet of the application of all the incomes of the Empire for discharge of responsibility.

LXXIII. In cases of extraordinary requirements, the contracting of a loan, also the undertaking of a guarantee on account of the Empire, may take place by Imperial legislation.

Final Stipulation to Section 12.

To the expenditure for the Bavarian Army Articles LXIX and LXXI are only applicable in conformity with the stipulations of the Treaty of November 23, 1870, mentioned in the final stipulation to Section 11, and Article LXXII only in so far that the assignment to Bavaria of the sums necessary for the Bavarian Army is to be notified to the Council of the Confederation and to the Imperial Diet.

13. Settlement of Differences and Penal Stipulations.

LXXIV. Every undertaking against the existence, the integrity, the safety, or the Constitution of the German Empire; finally, insulting the Council of the Confederation or the Imperial Diet, or a member of the Council of the Confederation or of the Imperial Diet, or any authority, or a public functionary of the Empire, whilst in the exercise of their vocation, or in reference to their vocation, by word, in writing, printing, drawing, figurative or other representation, will be sentenced and punished in the separate States of the Confederation according to the existing law, or the laws which may in future be enacted there, in pursuance of which a similar offence committed against that separate State of the Confederation, its Constitution, its Chambers, or Diet, the members of its Chambers or Diet, its authorities and functionaries would be punished.

LXXV. For those undertakings against the German Empire mentioned in Article LXXIV, which if they had been undertaken against one of the separate States of the Confederation would be qualified as high treason, or treason against the country, the Common Upper Court of Appeal of the three free and Hanseatic towns at Lübeck is the competent deciding authority in first and last instance.

The special regulations as to the competency and the procedure of the Upper Court of Appeal are to be settled by way of Imperial legislation. Until the promulgation of an Imperial law, the competency of the courts in the separate States of the Confederation and the provisions relative to the procedure of these courts remain as they have hitherto been.

LXXVI. Differences between various States of the Confederation, in so far as they are not of a private legal nature, and therefore to be decided by the competent judicial authorities, will, at the suit of one of the parties, be settled by the Council of the Confederation.

Constitutional differences in those States of the Confederation in whose constitution no authority for settling such disputes is provided are to be amicably arranged by the Council of the Confederation at the suit of one of the parties, or if this should not succeed, they are to be settled by way of Imperial legislation.

LXXVII. If, in a State of the Confederation, the case of a refusal of justice should occur, and sufficient aid cannot be obtained by way of law, it is the duty of the Council of the Confederation to take cognisance of the complaints as to the refused or hindered administration of the law when proved according to the Constitution and existing laws of the respective State of the Confederation, and thereupon to cause the Government of the Confederate State which has given occasion for the complaint to afford judicial aid.

14. General Stipulations.

LXXVIII. Alterations in the Constitution take place by way of legislation. They are considered as rejected if they have fourteen votes in the Council of the Confederation against them.

Those provisions of the Constitution of the Empire, by which certain rights are established for separate States of the Confederation in their relation to the community, can only be altered with the consent of the State of the Confederation entitled to those rights.

APPENDIX III

CHAPTER VII OF THE CONSTITUTION OF THE UNION OF SOCIALIST SOVIET REPUBLICS

The Supreme Court

Article 43.—In order to confirm revolutionary legality in the territory of the Union of Socialist Soviet Republics, there is set up, attached to the Central Executive Committee of the Union of Socialist Soviet Republics, a Supreme Court to whose competence it shall appertain:

(*a*) To give the Supreme Courts of the united republics guiding interpretations on questions of the general legislation of the Union.

(*b*) To examine and appeal to the Central Executive Committee of the Union of Socialist Soviet Republics, on the advice of the procurator of the Supreme Court of the Union of Socialist Soviet Republics, against resolutions, decisions and verdicts of the Supreme Courts of united republics on the ground of their being in contradiction to the general legislation of the Union, or in so far as they affect the interests of other republics.

(*c*) To give opinions at the demand of the Central Executive Committee of the Union of Socialist Soviet Republics as to the legality of resolutions of united republics from the point of view of the Constitution.

(*d*) To decide legal conflicts between united republics.

(*e*) To examine cases of accusations against the highest officials of the Union of Socialist Soviet Republics for offences committed in connection with their official duties.

ARTICLE 44.—The Supreme Court of the Union of Socialist Soviet Republics is composed of the following:

(*a*) The plenary session of the Supreme Court of the Union of Socialist Soviet Republics.

(*b*) The civil and criminal collegiums of the Supreme Court of the Union of Socialist Soviet Republics.

(*c*) The military and military transport collegiums.

ARTICLE 45.—The plenary session of the Supreme Court of the Union of Socialist Soviet

Republics consists of eleven members, including a president and his deputy, four presidents of plenary sessions of supreme courts of the united republics, and one representative of the United State Political Department of the Union of Socialist Soviet Republics, the president and his deputy and the remaining five members being appointed by the Presidium of the Central Executive Committee of the Union of Socialist Soviet Republics.

ARTICLE 46.—The procurator of the Supreme Court of the Union of Socialist Soviet Republics and his deputy are appointed by the Presidium of the Central Executive Committee of the Union of Socialist Soviet Republics. It lies with the procurator of the Supreme Court of the Union of Socialist Soviet Republics to give opinions on all questions subject to the decision of the Supreme Court of the Union of Socialist Soviet Republics, to support accusations at its sessions, and in case of non-agreement with the decision of the plenary session of the Supreme Court of the Union of Socialist Soviet Republics, to appeal to the Presidium of the Central Executive Committee of the Union of Socialist Soviet Republics.

ARTICLE 47.—The right of referring questions mentioned in Article 43 for examination by the plenary session of the Supreme Court of the Union of Socialist Soviet Republics is reserved solely to the initiative of the Central Executive Committee of the Union of Socialist Soviet Republics, its Presidium, the procurator of the Supreme Court of the Union of Socialist Soviet Republics, the procurators of the united republics and the United State Political Department of the Union of Socialist Republics.

ARTICLE 48.—Plenary sessions of the Supreme Court of the Union set up special legal tribunals (benches) for examination of:

(*a*) Criminal and civil cases of exceptional importance affecting by their nature two or more union republics; and

(*b*) Cases of the personal legal liabilities of members of the Central Executive Committee and Council of People's Commissaries of the Union of Socialist Soviet Republics.

The acceptance by the Supreme Court of the Union of Socialist Soviet Republics of these cases in its procedure can take place solely by special resolution, in each case, of the Central Executive Committee of the Union or its Presidium.

BIBLIOGRAPHY

ANONYMOUS: *The British Crown and the Indian States.* King and Sons, 1929.

BRUNET: *The German Constitution.* Fisher Unwin, 1923.

BRYCE: *American Commonwealth.* 2 vols. Macmillan, new edition, 1911.

BRYCE: *Modern Democracies.* Macmillan, 1921.

BRYCE: *Studies in History and Jurisprudence.* 2 vols. Oxford University Press, 1901.

BRYCE: *Holy Roman Empire.* Macmillan, 1889.

CLEMENT: *Law of the Canadian Constitution.* Sweet and Maxwell.

COXE: *Judicial Power and Unconstitutional Legislation.* Philadelphia, 1893.

DICEY: *The Law of the Constitution.* Macmillan, 8th edition.

HAINES: *American Doctrine of Judicial Supremacy.*

HALL: *International Law*, 8th (Higgins') edition.

HAMILTON: *The Federalist.*

HEWART: *The New Despotism.* Benn, 1929.

ILBERT: *The Government of India.* Oxford University Press, 1922.

JAMES: *Federal Constitution of Germany.* Annals of the American Academy of Political Science, 1890.

KEITH: *Responsible Government in the Dominions.* Second edition, Oxford, 1928.

KEITH: *Sovereignty of the British Dominions.* Macmillan.

KEITH: *Constitutions and Laws of the Empire.* Collins, 1924.

KENT: *Commentaries* (Holmes' edition).

LOWELL: *Parties and Politics in Continental Governments.* Macmillan.

MOSES: *The Federal Government of Switzerland.* Longmans, 1927.

NICHOLSON: *Scraps of Paper*. Benn, 1930.

PANIKKAR: *Indian States and the Government of India*. Martin Hopkinson, 1927.

PANIKKAR (KERALA PUTRA): *The Working of Dyarchy in India*. Bombay, 1928.

PANIKKAR: *The Evolution of British Policy towards the States*. Calcutta, 1929.

POLITIS: *Les nouvelles tendences du droit international*. Hachette, Paris, 1927.

POURRA ET PIERRE: *Traité du droit politique*. Paris.

PRASAD: *The Indian Constitution*. Allahabad, 1928.

QUICK AND GARRAN: *The Commonwealth of Australia*, 1901.

QUICK: *Legislative Powers of the Commonwealth of Australia*. Maxwell, Chancery Lane, Melbourne, 1919.

RIDDEL: *The Canadian Constitution in Form and Fact*. Columbia University Lectures.

SIVASWAMY: *The Indian Constitutional Problem*. Bombay, 1928.

TUPPER: *Our Indian Protectorate*. Longmans, 1893.

VENABLE: *The Partition of Powers between the Federal and the State Governments*.

LEE-WARNER: *The Native States of India*. Macmillan, 1910.

WHYTE: *India : A Federation?* Government of India Press, 1925.

WILSON: *The State*. Harrap, 1919.

REPORTS.

Report of the Indian States Committee, 1929. H.M. Stationery Office.

Report of the All-Parties Conference. Allahabad, 1928.

Report of the Proceedings of the Chamber of Princes, 1930.

PRINTED IN GREAT BRITAIN BY BILLING AND SONS LTD., GUILDFORD AND ESHER